MANUAL OF MODERN RUSSIAN PROSE C
(MODERN RUSSIAN USAGE)

MODERN RUSSIAN PROSE COMPOSITION

BOOK ONE (passages for translation into Russian — intermediate)
BOOK TWO (passages for translation into Russian — advanced)
MANUAL (MODERN RUSSIAN USAGE)

Manual of Modern Russian Prose Composition (Modern Russian Usage)

PETER HENRY, M.A.

Professor in the Department of Slavonic Languages and Literature, University of Glasgow

HODDER AND STOUGHTON
LONDON SYDNEY AUCKLAND TORONTO

ISBN 0 340 15170 6

First published 1963
Second edition: fifth impression 1979
Copyright © P. Henry 1966

Printed in Great Britain for
Hodder and Stoughton Educational,
a division of Hodder and Stoughton Ltd,
Mill Road, Dunton Green, Sevenoaks, Kent,
by Hazell Watson & Viney Ltd, Aylesbury, Bucks

Preface

This volume is intended as a practical reference book for use when writing Russian compositions and translating passages into Russian. It does not claim to be a comprehensive account of Russian grammar and syntax of the type to be found in such standard works as *Russian Grammar* by B. O. Unbegaun and *Russian Syntax* by F. M. Borras and R. F. Christian. The aim has been to provide a guide for the writing of correct Russian and the range has been restricted to what may safely be said or written by the student of Russian; thus the book is not a collection of the rarer points of usage which may be encountered in one's reading.

The basic parts of speech and syntax are dealt with, the emphasis being on those topics that cause difficulties to the English student, e.g. cases of nouns and adjectives in the predicate, tenses, aspects, participles and gerunds, conditionals, verbs of motion, verbs such as 'to put', the negative, prepositions, expressions of time, conjunctions, etc. Owing to the difficulties they present, numerals are dealt with fully, including their declension. There is also a section on such prosaic matters as punctuation, the use of capitals and the transcription of English names, on which there is little information available in English textbooks. At the end of the book there is a section on the translation of certain English words which often cause difficulty.

Wherever possible, lengthy theoretical explanations have been avoided; instead, points have been illustrated by examples drawn as far as possible from practical, everyday Russian and based on a minimum vocabulary.

Originally the material contained in this volume had been intended as an Appendix to the annotated proses of Modern Russian Prose Composition, which have been published in two separate volumes, and in which many of the Notes refer to the relevant sections of this book. However, this Manual has been enlarged to form a reference book in its own right.

The author gratefully acknowledges the help given by the following: Professor Nadejda Gorodetzky, M.A., B.Litt., D.Phil., who read an early version of the manuscript and made a number of valuable suggestions; members of the A.T.R. Textbook Committee, many of whose suggestions were incorporated in the final version; and J. Forsyth, M.A., Head of the Department of Russian, Aberdeen University, who helped to eliminate several inaccuracies and obscurities. The author's greatest single debt is to S. A. Khavronina of Friendship University, Moscow, who checked the Russian of the manuscript at an advanced stage and made many important contributions. Among members of the staff of МГУ who gave assistance on specific points are Professor D. E. Rozental' and G. I. Rozhkova. O. P. Rassudova provided material on the classification and usage of aspects that was drawn upon in preparing §§97-101.

In this second edition a number of minor additions and alterations have been made, particularly in the sections on Verbal Aspects, Verbs of Motion and Expressions of Time.

P.H.

Sources consulted:

«Толковый словарь русского языка» под ред. Д. Н. Ушакова. ОГИЗ, М. 1935-1940.

«Словарь современного русского литературного языка». АН СССР, М.-Л., 1950-.

«Русское литературное произношение и ударение» под ред. Р. И. Аванесова и С. И. Ожегова. ГИС, М., 1959.

«Грамматика русского языка». АН СССР, М., 1954.

«Культура речи», Д. Э. Розенталь. Из-во Московского университета, М., 1959.

«Основы перевода», Н. Б. Аристов. Из-во литературы на иностранных языках, М., 1959.

«Основы перевода с английского языка на русский», С. С. Толстой. Из-во ИМО, М., 1957.

Recommended further reading:

B. O. UNBEGAUN, *Russian Grammar*. Oxford University Press, 1957.

F. M. BORRAS and R. F. CHRISTIAN, *Russian Syntax*. Oxford University Press, 1959.

I. M. PULKINA, *A Short Russian Reference Grammar*. FLPH, Moscow, 1960.

А. Н. Гвоздев, «Очерки по стилистике русского языка». Учпедгиз, М., 1955.

А. М. Земский, С. Е. Крючков, М. В. Светлаев, «Русский язык» (2 тт.). Учпедгиз, М., 1954.

Д. Э. Розенталь и В. А. Добромыслов, «Трудные вопросы грамматики и правописания». Учпедгиз, М., 1955; 2-я серия, 1960.

Contents

CONTENTS

Abbreviations used

acc.	accusative	*infin.*	infinitive
adj.	adjective	*instr.*	instrumental
adv.	adverb	*lit.*	literally
cf.	compare	*m.*	masculine
coll.	colloquial	*n.*	neuter
comp.	comparative	*orig.*	originally
compd. conj.	compound con-	*pass.*	passive
	junction	*past part. pass.*	past participle
conj.	conjunction		passive
dat.	dative	*pers.*	person
f.	feminine	*pfv.*	perfective
fut. pfv.	future perfective	*pl.*	plural
gen.	genitive	*prep.*	prepositional
gen. pl.	genitive plural	*pres.*	present
gen. sing.	genitive singular	*pres. part. pass.*	present participle
imp.	imperative		passive
impers.	impersonal	*prp.*	preposition
impfv.	imperfective	*sing.*	singular
indecl.	indeclinable	*vb.*	verb

Word Division, Capitals, Punctuation, Word Order

DIVISION OF WORDS BY SYLLABLES

§1 If a word is to be divided at the end of a line, the following points should be noted:

A consonant should not be separated from the following vowel:

лю-бо́вь	ре-бя́-га	па-сту́х (пас-ту́х)

However, prefixes ending on a consonant are best left intact:

без-у́мный	rather than	бе-зу́мный
раз-очаро́ван	rather than	ра-зочаро́ван

ъ remains with the prefix and -й with the preceding vowel:

подъ-е́зд	объ-явле́ние	май-о́р

Double consonants are separated:

ма́с-са	напи́сан-ный	сож-жён-ный

Endings such as **-ный**, **-ский** are best separated from the stem:

шу́м-ный	rather than	шу́-мный
интере́с-ный	rather than	интере́-сный
ру́с-ский	rather than	ру́сс-кий
англи́й-ский	rather than	англи́йс-кий

CAPITALS

§2 Russian is much more sparing in the use of capitals than English. Days, months, titles, professions, etc. are written without capital letters:

понеде́льник	янва́рь	това́рищ Со́мов
граф Толсто́й	ста́рший инжене́р (*Chief Engineer*)	

The word **бог**, *God*, is now also written with a small letter:

бог	бо́же мой

Points of the compass are written with small initials:

се́вер	юг	восто́к	за́пад

So, too, are nouns and adjectives indicating nationality, as well as adjectives formed from geographical names:

англича́нин   англи́йская шко́ла   ло́ндонские у́лицы

§3 With geographical names, street names, names of buildings and institutions, etc. the classifying noun (e.g. 'Sea' in Black Sea) begins with a small letter, and the descriptive noun or adjective ('Black' Sea) with a capital:

река́ Москва́, Москва́-река́	*the River Moskva*
Моско́вская о́бласть	*Moscow District*
Мохова́я у́лица	*Mokhovaya Street*
Кра́сная пло́щадь	*Red Square*
Ма́лый теа́тр	*the Maly Theatre*
Моско́вский госуда́рственный университе́т	*Moscow State University*
Брита́нский музе́й	*the British Museum*

§4 With names of countries, each word begins with a capital letter:

Украи́нская Сове́тская Социали́стическая Респу́блика	*the Ukrainian Soviet Socialist Republic*
Соединённые Шта́ты	*the United States*

§5 In the case of historic events, public holidays, etc., as with geographical names, the noun begins with a small letter and the adjective with a capital:

Верса́льский догово́р	*the Treaty of Versailles*
Вели́кая Оте́чественная война́	*the Great Patriotic War*
Но́вый год	*New Year*
Пе́рвое ма́я	*the First of May*

PUNCTUATION

THE COMMA

§6 The main difficulty of Russian punctuation lies in the use of the comma (запята́я). It is used much more precisely in Russian than in English. It does not merely indicate a pause (cf. in English: 'After a while, we decided to go on.'); it is not used in Russian unless there is a syntactical reason for it.

§7 The comma is used when enumerating words of the same category:

Стоя́ла прекра́сная, споко́йная, хотя́ не о́чень тёплая пого́да.
The weather was beautiful and calm, though not very warm.

The use of *and* before the last item in a list of words is less common in Russian than in English:

В ко́мнате всё вы́глядело ую́тно, чи́сто, светло́.
Everything in the room looked cosy, clean and light.

When **а** and **но** link two complete main clauses (each with subject and verb), they are preceded by a comma:

Она́ чита́ла кни́гу, а брат писа́л письмо́.
She was reading a book and her brother was writing a letter.

Со́лнце уже́ зашло́ за го́ры, но бы́ло ещё светло́.
The sun had already sunk behind the hills, but it was still light.

A comma is also used before **но** when two words are contrasted:

Он был умён, но лени́в.
He was intelligent but lazy.

§8 Commas are used *invariably* to mark off subordinate clauses, whether they are relative, conditional, causal, or temporal:

Я не понима́ю, что вы говори́те.
I do not understand what you are saying.

Я не зна́ю, где он живёт.
I do not know where he lives.

Скажи́те, пожа́луйста, кото́рый час.
Tell me the time, please.

Он сказа́л, что уже́ по́здно.
He said that it was late.

Я пойду́ с ва́ми, е́сли бу́дет вре́мя.
I'll go with you if I have time.

Он смотре́л, как пти́цы лета́ют по не́бу.
He watched the birds flying in the sky.

A conjunction followed by an infinitive is normally preceded by a comma. This rule does not apply to plain infinitives, e.g. those following verbs of motion:

Я не зна́ю, что де́лать.
I don't know what to do.

15

Я пришёл с тем, чтобы помо́чь вам.

I have come in order to help you.

Я пришёл помо́чь вам.

I have come to help you.

Она́ пошла́ купи́ть но́вое пла́тье.

She went to buy a new dress.

A comma is also used in comparisons:

Он тако́й же у́мный, как она́.

He is as intelligent as she.

Лу́чше по́здно, чем никогда́.

Better late than never.

§9 Participle and gerund clauses, as well as adjectives in apposition, are also separated from the rest of the sentence by commas:

Го́ры, покры́тые сне́гом, блесте́ли на у́треннем со́лнце.

The snow-covered mountains gleamed in the morning sun.

Погружённый в свои́ мы́сли, он ничего́ не отве́тил.

Absorbed in his thoughts, he did not answer.

Неда́вно я узна́л, что Печо́рин, возвраща́ясь из Пе́рсии, у́мер.

[Ле́рмонтов]

Not long ago I learned that Pechorin had died on his way back from Persia.

По́сле экза́менов она́, весёлая и бо́драя, верну́лась домо́й на ле́то.

After the examinations she returned home for the summer, cheerful and bright.

Sometimes, however, the gerund is closely associated with the verb, in which case no comma is used:

Он ку́рит не переставая.　　　　*He smokes incessantly.*

§10 Certain words and phrases that are used parenthetically are also separated off by commas. They include **пожа́луйста, спаси́бо, наприме́р, кро́ме, в том числе́, то есть, коне́чно, ка́жется, пра́вда, ме́жду про́чим**:

Мно́гие ру́сские поэ́ты, наприме́р Жуко́вский, бы́ли отли́чными перево́дчиками.

Many Russian poets, for example Zhukovsky, were excellent translators.

16

Кро́ме меня́ и до́ктора, у неё в го́роде не́ было никаки́х зна-ко́мых.

Apart from the doctor and me she had no acquaintances in town.

Вы, коне́чно, пра́вы.

Of course you are right.

Да́йте, пожа́луйста, воды́.

Give me some water, please.

Да and **нет** (*yes, no*) are separated from the rest of the sentence by commas.

§11 PUNCTUATION WITH DIRECT STATEMENTS

Inverted commas (кавы́чки) are written „ " and printed « ».

«Кто там?» — «Я.»   *'Who is there?' 'It's me.'*

The dash (тире́) is used:

(i) To separate two direct statements (as above);

(ii) Before and after *he said, he asked,* etc. if these are inserted or follow the direct statement:

Он сказа́л: «Уже́ по́здно, нам пора́ идти́.»

«Уже́ по́здно, — сказа́л он, — нам пора́ идти́.»

«Уже́ по́здно, нам пора́ идти́», — сказа́л он.

«Здра́вствуйте, Ива́н Па́влович! — сказа́л я. — Как вы пожива́ете?»

Note that inverted commas occur only twice, once at the beginning and once at the very end of the statement.

§12 The dash is also used:

(i) When the verb **быть** is omitted, particularly in definitive statements where both the subject and its complement are nouns:

Ло́ндон — столи́ца А́нглии.   *London is the capital of England.*

Пионе́р — всем де́тям приме́р.   *A Pioneer is an example for all children.*

Мой брат — учи́тель.   *My brother is a teacher.*

but:

Мой брат ста́рше меня́.   *My brother is older than I.*

Он учи́тель.   *He is a teacher.*

It is not used with **не**, *is not*:

Мой брат не учи́тель.   *My brother is not a teacher.*

17

(ii) When the complement is an infinitive:

Долг си́льного — помога́ть сла́бому.
It is the duty of the strong to help the weak.

Жизнь прожи́ть — не по́ле перейти́.
To live one's life is not as simple as a walk across a field.

(iii) When э́то or вот is interpolated:

Спу́тник — э́то вели́кое нау́чное достиже́ние.
The sputnik is a great scientific achievement.

See also §123.

(iv) In sentences consisting of two main clauses, the second of which is incomplete:

Мы живём в це́нтре го́рода, а он — на окра́ине.
We live in the centre of town, and he (lives) on the outskirts.

WORD ORDER

Russian word order is flexible. Its correct use is important, not only from the point of view of style and emphasis (see, for example, §74, ii), but also because a change in word order can involve a change in meaning.

§13 As in English, the simple sentence normally follows the order Subject — Verb — Object/Complement:

Мой оте́ц рабо́тает инжене́ром на большо́м заво́де.
My father works as an engineer in a big factory.

На днях я чита́л интере́сную кни́гу о Росси́и.
The other day I was reading an interesting book about Russia.

§14 The subject is often placed at the end, when this is a new person or factor being introduced:

За э́тим заня́тием он не слы́шал, как в ко́мнату вошёл оте́ц.
While thus occupied, he did not hear his father enter the room.

This applies in particular when rendering the English indefinite article:

Кни́га на столе́.	*The book is on the table.*
На столе́ кни́га.	*There is a book on the table.*
Стари́к сиде́л в ко́мнате.	*The old man was sitting in the room.*
В ко́мнате сиде́л стари́к.	*An old man was sitting in the room.*

See also §81.

This word order is also common when an English passive is expressed by a Russian active verb (see §109):

Дверь открыл мальчик.   *The door was opened by a boy.*

§15 English tends to put the most important word or words first, with attendant circumstances following in order of decreasing importance:

An accident occurred in the Physics Laboratory at three o'clock yesterday.

Russian starts with the less significant and gradually builds up in a steadily rising curve, culminating in the most important element, placed last in the sentence:

Вчера (approximate time), в три часа (specific time), в физической лаборатории (place) произошёл (verb) несчастный случай (subject and emphasised element).

Вдали, за рекой, виднелся огромный тёмный лес.
A huge dark forest could be seen beyond the river in the distance.

Expressions of time and place are commonly placed at the beginning:

Вчера вечером мы ходили в кино.
We went to the cinema last night.

У нас в городе несколько театров.
There are several theatres in our town.

See also §121.

§16 The normal position of the adverb is immediately before the verb:

Я очень люблю музыку.   *I like music very much.*

Мой отец сильно постарел.   *My father had aged considerably.*

Мы хорошо поговорили.   *We had a good talk.*

Она внимательно смотрела на него.   *She looked at him attentively.*

Он хорошо говорит по-русски.   *He speaks Russian well.*

An adverb standing at the beginning or the end of a sentence, i.e. not in its normal position, is emphasised:

Он говорит очень интересно.
What he says is very interesting.

Мы говори́ли до́лго, почти́ до полу́ночи.
We talked for a long time, almost until midnight.

По-ру́сски он говори́т хорошо́, по-неме́цки же — нева́жно.
He speaks Russian well, but German not so well.

нача́ть жить по-но́вому
to begin a new life

Недаром весь мир бои́тся но́вой войны́.
The whole world has every reason (lit. *not without reason*) *to fear another war.*

INVERSION OF SUBJECT AND COMPLEMENT

§17 Inversion frequently occurs when the subject is the important or unexpected element (see §15):

Причи́ной э́того недоразуме́ния явля́ется их неспосо́бность поня́ть на́шу то́чку зре́ния.
The reason for this misunderstanding is their inability to see our point of view.

Similarly:

When Kutuzov was appointed Commander-in-Chief, the morale of the Russian army rose immediately.

The emphasis here is not so much on the fact that Kutuzov was promoted, but that now there was a new Commander-in-Chief, namely Kutuzov:

Когда́ главнокома́ндующим был назна́чен Куту́зов, дух ру́сской а́рмии сра́зу подня́лся.

Sometimes it is difficult to determine the subject in sentences of the following type:

Our first Russian teacher was a Pole.

One must see which is the permanent characteristic (*Pole*) and which the temporary occupation (*teacher*):

На́шим пе́рвым учи́телем ру́сского языка́ был поля́к.

До войны́ столи́цей Герма́нии был Берли́н.
Before the war Berlin was the capital of Germany.

See also §27.

§18 In the middle or at the end of a direct statement the words *he said, he asked,* etc. are inverted:

«Куда́ вы идёте?» — спроси́ла она́. — «Я иду́ в го́род, — отве́тил он, — но я ско́ро верну́сь.»

'Where are you going?' she asked. 'I'm going to town,' he answered, 'but I shall be back soon.'

§19 WORD ORDER IN QUESTIONS

(i) No inversion is necessary with a question. The difference between «Э́то ва́ша кни́га» (*This is your book*) and «Э́то ва́ша кни́га?» (*Is this your book?*) is brought out in speech by intonation:

Вы э́то чита́ли?	*Have you read this?*
Вы чита́ли э́то?	

But changes in word order are possible and common:

Э́то вы чита́ли?   *Is THIS what you read?*

With ли inversion is normal, the verb being placed first in the sentence:

Вы его́ зна́ете?	*Do you know him?*
Зна́ете ли вы его́?	

The question may also begin with another emphasised word:

Вы ли э́то сде́лали?   *Was it YOU who did this?*

Ли is normally used with negative questions with inverted word order:

Вы э́того не зна́ете?	*Do you not know this?*
Не зна́ете ли вы э́того?	

After an interrogative word the rest of the question is as a rule not inverted:

Кто э́то сде́лал?	*Who did this?*
Куда́ вы идёте?	*Where are you going?*
Почему́ вы не пришли́?	*Why did you not come?*

(ii) **Ра́зве** and **неуже́ли** introduce an element of surprise, anxiety or doubt into the question, **неуже́ли** being the more emphatic:

Ра́зве он придёт?	*Is he really coming?* (Surprise)
Неуже́ли э́то он?	*That can't be him, surely.* (Surprise and doubt)
Неуже́ли вы э́того не зна́ли?	*Fancy your not knowing that!* (Surprise and incredulity)
Ра́зве я говорю́ непра́вду?	*I'm not telling a lie, you know.* (Indignant assertion)

See also §199.

The Noun

§20 COMMON GENDER

There are occupations in which both men and women are engaged (teacher, doctor, secretary, engineer, conductor, driver, etc.). For some of these Russian has a special feminine form:

ученик — ученица   учитель — учительница

студент — студентка   секретарь — секретарша

тракторист — трактористка

NOTE: Машинист is *engine-driver*, машинистка, *typist*.

The ending -ша in some cases denotes a feminine agent, in others it has the meaning *the wife of*:

билетёрша, кондукторша = *usherette, conductress*

докторша, профессорша = жена доктора, жена профессора

With many nouns it is common to use the masculine form when describing a feminine agent:

Кондуктор сидела (ог кондукторша сидела) у входа.[1]
The conductress was sitting by the entrance.

Лекцию читал/читала профессор Тарасевич.
The lecture was delivered by Professor Tarasevich (may be m. or f.).[2]

Она была хороший человек.
She was a good person.

Она мой большой друг.
She is a great friend of mine.

See also §32.

---

[1] A masculine verb MAY be used (кондуктор сидел . . .), but not where it is clear that the subject is feminine: кондуктор Иванова сидела . . .

[2] Most Russian surnames have both a masculine and feminine form: Алексей Александрович Каренин, Анна Аркадьевна Каренина; Толстой, Толстая; but non-Russian names have only one form: Павленко (Ukrainian), Цпранкевич (Polish), Джонсон (English).

Товáрищ, *comrade,* is used with the surname of both men and women:

Товáрищ Соколóв сидéл в клýбе.

Товáрищ Соколóва сидéла в клýбе.

It is also used for *Ladies and Gentlemen* (**Товáрищи**) and it is used generally of Soviet citizens:

Э́тот товáрищ тóлько что вы́шел/вы́шла.
This person has just gone out.

Извини́те, товáрищ.   *Excuse me, Sir.*

CASES

§21 THE ACCUSATIVE

For the accusative in expressions of time, see §163.

For its use in negative statements, see §§143-4.

The Accusative of Animate Nouns

The accusative (singular and plural) of MASCULINE nouns denoting animate beings is identical with the genitive form:

Я знáю вáшего брáта (вáших брáтьев).
I know your brother (brothers).

Мы ви́дели мáльчика (мáльчиков).
We saw a boy (boys).

Скáзка про Ивáна-царéвича.
The tale about Ivan the Tsarevich.

Мы ви́дели вóлка (волкóв).
We saw a wolf (wolves).

The accusative of FEMININE animate nouns coincides with the genitive form in the plural only:

Я знáю вáшу сестрý (вáших сестёр).
I know your sister (sisters).

Я встрéтил вáшу мать.
I met your mother.

Онá лю́бит э́ту собáку (собáк).
She is fond of this dog (of dogs).

The same also applies to the few NEUTER nouns denoting animate beings, e.g. **существó,** *a being;* **лицó,** *person;* **живóтное,** *animal:*

Онá óчень лю́бит э́то живóтное (живóтных).
She is very fond of this animal (of animals).

23

This use of the genitive form applies only to nouns denoting individual persons or beings; it does not apply to collective nouns, e.g. **наро́д**, *a people*; **полк**, *regiment*; **скот**, *cattle*:

Он лю́бит ру́сских.	*He loves the Russians.*
Он лю́бит ру́сский наро́д.	*He loves the Russian people.*
Пора́ корми́ть коро́в.	*It is time to feed the cows.*
Пора́ корми́ть скот.	*It is time to feed the cattle.*

Те́ло, *body*, and **труп**, *corpse*, are treated as inanimate nouns; **мертве́ц**, *dead person*; **поко́йник**, *the deceased*, as animate:

В му́тной воде́ рыбаки́ обнару́жили труп (мертвеца́).
The fishermen found a body (dead person) in the dark water.

Тип, *type, fellow (coll.)* and **член**, *limb, member*, may be animate or inanimate according to the context; **о́браз**, *image* or *character* (in a book), is inanimate:

В База́рове Турге́нев со́здал но́вый литерату́рный тип (ог но́вый литерату́рный о́браз, but но́вого литерату́рного геро́я).
In Bazarov Turgenev created a new literary type (character, hero).
Contrast:

Вы зна́ете э́того ти́па? — Нет, не вида́л его́.
Do you know this fellow? No, I have never seen him.

Note the use of the inanimate accusative plural in the following expression:

Он вы́шел в лю́ди.	*He rose in the world.*
Его́ произвели́ в сержа́нты.	*He was promoted to the rank of sergeant.*

In such expressions **в** with the accusative (or prepositional) indicates membership of a specific social group or profession:

в лю́дях	*in the world*
попа́сть в актёры	*to become an actor*
поступи́ть в дво́рники	
служи́ть в дво́рниках	*to become, be, a janitor*

§22 THE GENITIVE

For the translation of *of*, see §157.
For the genitive in negative statements, see §§141-145.
For the genitive of comparison, see §52.

Some masculine nouns have two forms of the genitive singular, the normal one (ending in -a, -я) and another form (ending in -y, -ю). The latter is used:

(i) In some partitive expressions (see §81), e.g.

мёд	honey	фунт мёду	a pound of honey
мел	chalk	кусок мелу	a piece of chalk
сахар	sugar	фунт сахару	a pound of sugar
суп	soup	тарелка супу	a plate of soup
сыр	cheese	кусок сыру	a piece of cheese
чай	tea	стакан чаю	a glass of tea

So also:

купить мёду (сахару, сыру)   to buy some honey (sugar, cheese)

Note also **много народу**, *many people*; **мало толку**, *little sense*; **много шуму из ничего**, *much ado about nothing*, etc.
But:

чай без сахара	tea without sugar
продажа чая	sale of tea
вкус мёда	taste of honey
тарелка для супа	soup plate
сын народа	son of the people

In these cases no partitive notion is present.

(ii) In certain negative expressions, e.g.

Не было чаю.	There was no tea.
Не выпало снегу.	There has been no snow.
Он не пришёл ни разу.	Not once did he come.
О нём ни слуху ни духу.	There has been no news of him.
Не выйдет толку из этого.	Nothing will come of it.

(iii) In certain idiomatic prepositional phrases, in particular with из and до, e.g. **из дому, из лесу, до дому**:

Мы вышли из дому рано утром.[1]	We left home early in the morning.
До дому ещё далеко.[1]	We are still a long way from home.
Мы потеряли его из виду.	We lost sight of him.

[1] **Мы вышли из дома** means *we left the house*, до дома, *as far as the house* (here *from the house*). When the noun is qualified, the normal genitive form is used: из нашего дома, до его дома, фунт китайского чая.

Note also:

с бóку нá бок	*from side to side*
час óт часу	*hour after hour*
до чáсу	*till one o'clock*
бéз толку	*senselessly*

Óтроду, óт роду (lit. *since birth*):

Óтроду не слыхáл такóй вздор.　　*Never in my life have I heard such nonsense.*

Емý двáдцать лет óт роду.　　*He is twenty years of age.*

Note the movement of the stress on to the preposition in most of these expressions.

§23　THE DATIVE

For the dative in impersonal expressions, see §§137-9.
For the use of the dative and infinitive, see §150.
For the dative in statements of age, see §68.

After verbs like **давáть/дать**, *to give*; **говорúть/сказáть**, *to say, tell*; **отвечáть/отвéтить**, *to answer*; **писáть/на-**, *to write*, the recipient is expressed by the plain dative. **Посылáть/послáть** is used with **к** (+ *dat.*) when the object is a person.

Compare:

Он послáл дирéктору запúску.
He sent a note to the Headmaster.

Он послáл мáльчика к дирéктору.
He sent the boy to the Headmaster.

§24　THE INSTRUMENTAL

The instrumental is used:

(i) For the means by which an action is performed:

На э́том завóде тепéрь почтú всё дéлается машúнами.
At this factory almost everything is now done by machines.

Он рéзал хлеб ножóм.
He cut the loaf with a knife.

éхать пóездом, автóбусом и т. д.
to travel by train, by bus, etc.

26

(ii) To translate *by way of, along*:

Влади́мир е́хал бе́регом широ́кой реки́.
Vladimir was riding along the bank of a broad river.

Доро́га шла леса́ми и поля́ми.
The road led through forests and fields.

Cf. §156.

(iii) For the manner in which an action is performed, in comparisons, similes, etc.:

Он шёл по доро́ге нетвёрдыми шага́ми (нетвёрдой похо́дкой).
He walked unsteadily along the road.

Они́ шли отде́льными гру́ппами.
They went in separate groups.

Со́лнце заходи́ло; его́ после́дние лучи́ широ́кими полоса́ми распространя́лись по не́бу.
The sun was setting, its last rays spreading in broad shafts over the sky.

Уби́тая пти́ца ка́мнем упа́ла вниз.
The shot bird fell like a stone.

Note:

Они́ стоя́ли к нам спино́й.
They stood with their backs to us.

Он вско́ре засну́л кре́пким сном.
Soon he was fast asleep.

(iv) For the agent with passive verbs:

Э́та карти́на напи́сана молоды́м францу́зским худо́жником.
This picture was painted by a young French artist.

Прави́тельством был и́здан но́вый ука́з (декре́т).
A new decree was issued by the government.

(v) In impersonal statements with a passive meaning:

Бе́рег за́лило водо́й.   *The shore was flooded with water.*

Облака́ми покры́ло не́бо.   *Dark clouds covered the sky.*

See also §§26-31 (nouns in the predicate), 44-5 (predicative adjectives), 105-110 (passive participles and passive verbs), 158 (translation of *with*), 162 (expressions of time).

§25 THE PREPOSITIONAL (LOCATIVE)

The prepositional of a number of masculine nouns, mainly mono-syllabics, ends in -ý (-ю́): сад (*garden*), в саду́; бой (*battle, fight*), в бою́. This ending only occurs after в and на.

Other examples:

бал	*dance*	на балу́
бе́рег	*bank, coast*	на берегу́
бок	*side*	на боку́
год	*year*	в году́
долг	*debt*	в долгу́
жар	*heat, fever*	в жару́
край	*edge; land, region*	на краю́; в краю́
лёд	*ice*	во/на льду
лес	*forest*	в лесу́
лоб	*forehead*	во/на лбу
луг	*meadow*	на лугу́
мост	*bridge*	на мосту́
нос	*nose*	в/на носу́
плен	*captivity*	в плену́
пол	*floor*	на полу́
полк	*regiment*	в полку́
пруд	*pond*	в/на пруду́
рот	*mouth*	во рту
ряд	*row*	в ряду́
снег	*snow*	в/на снегу́
у́гол	*corner*	в/на углу́
цвет	*flower*	в цвету́
шкаф	*cupboard, wardrobe*	в/на шкафу́
Дон	*Don*	на Дону́
Крым	*Crimea*	в Крыму́

Note, however: о са́де, при са́де, о полке́, при полке́, etc.

Similarly, a few feminine nouns of the -ь type have two forms of the prepositional: -и and -и́, e.g. грязь (*mud*), в грязи́ (*covered in mud, in the mud*), and о гря́зи (*about the mud*).

Other examples:

даль	distance	в дали
дверь	door	в двери (*in the doorway*)
кровь	blood	в крови (*covered in blood*)
печь	stove	в/на печи
пыль	dust	в пыли (*covered in dust*)
степь	steppe	в степи

PREDICATIVE NOMINATIVE AND INSTRUMENTAL

I. AS COMPLEMENT OF быть

§26 Both cases are found in the predicate after **быть**. Broadly speaking, their functions differ in that the nominative expresses a permanent or the most significant characteristic of the subject, while the instrumental describes a temporary state or occupation.

In the present tense, however, only the nominative is used, fulfilling both these functions:

Сергей — брат Сони.	*Sergei is Sonya's brother.*
Тепе́рь он студе́нт.	*He is now a student.*
Мой люби́мый предме́т — исто́рия.	*My favourite subject is History.*
Москва́ — столи́ца СССР.	*Moscow is the capital of the U.S.S.R.*

These statements are wholly true at the time the statement is made and the subject and complement can be said to be the two elements of an equation. (For the use of the dash, see §12.)

§27 In the past tense one must distinguish between two types of statements — those which are only true of a limited period of time (*At that time he was a student*), and those which express permanent characteristics or are summary pronouncements on the subject (*Sergei was Sonya's brother. Pushkin was a great poet.*):

Тогда́ он был **студе́нтом**.	Серге́й был **брат Со́ни**.
Пу́шкин был **вели́кий поэ́т**.	

Бопре́ в оте́честве своём был парикма́хером, пото́м в Пру́ссии солда́том. [Пу́шкин]

In his native country Beauprés had been a barber, then a soldier in Prussia.

Моим люби́мым предме́том была́ исто́рия.
My favourite subject was History.

В девятна́дцатом ве́ке столи́цей Росси́йской Импе́рии был Санкт-Петербу́рг.
In the nineteenth century St Petersburg was the capital of the Russian Empire.

Для неё бы́ло сюрпри́зом, когда́...
It was (came as) a surprise for her, when...

Уже́ давно́ мое́й мечто́й бы́ло посети́ть Пари́ж.
I had long dreamt of visiting Paris.

In the last four sentences the complement precedes the subject; see also §17.

Both the nominative and the instrumental can be used to express the profession held by a person throughout his adult life (but see § 28):

Че́хов был не то́лько писа́тель и драмату́рг, но и врач (писа́телем... драмату́ргом... врачо́м).
Chekhov was not only a writer and dramatist, but also a doctor.

§28 The tendency in modern Russian is to use the instrumental in the past tense where in the nineteenth century the nominative would have been used (i.e. to describe a permanent state). Contrast:

Сабу́ров был вполне́ **челове́ком** своего́ поколе́ния. [Си́монов]
Saburov was entirely a man of his generation (i.e. *typical of his generation*).

Степа́н Арка́дьич был **челове́к правди́вый** в отноше́нии к себе́ самому́. [Л. Н. Толсто́й]
Stepan Arkadich had no illusions about himself (lit. *was a truthful person in relation to himself*).

§29 With the future tense the instrumental is used invariably, since the statement cannot have the force of an established fact:

Он бу́дет инжене́ром (врачо́м и т. д.).
He is going to be an engineer (doctor, etc.).

И бу́дешь ты цари́цей ми́ра,
Подру́га пе́рвая моя́.   [Ле́рмонтов]
And Thou shalt be the Queen of the world, Thou my first beloved one.

§30 The instrumental of the noun is normally used with the infinitive, imperative and gerund (**быть, будь/бу́дьте, бу́дучи**):

Он реши́л быть пило́том.   *He decided to be a pilot.*

30

Будь мужчи́ной! *Be a man!*

Бу́дучи о́пытным пило́том, он суме́л сде́лать благополу́чную поса́дку.
Being an experienced pilot he succeeded in landing the plane safely.

II. WITH OTHER LINK VERBS

§31 Link verbs whose functions are similar to that of **быть**, e.g. **явля́ться, каза́ться/по–, ока́зываться/оказа́ться, станови́ться/ стать, де́латься/с–, счита́ть(ся)**, are always used with the instrumental, i.e. also in the present. **Служи́ть, рабо́тать** can also be used in this way:

Причи́ной явля́ется то, что . . .
The reason is that . . .

Он каза́лся интере́сным челове́ком.
He seemed to be an interesting person.

Он стал актёром.
He became an actor.

Он счита́ется (его́ счита́ют) хоро́шим актёром.
He is considered to be a good actor.

Мой оте́ц рабо́тает инжене́ром.
My father is (works as) an engineer.

Он служи́л сержа́нтом.
He was (served as) a sergeant.

See also §45.

NOUNS IN APPOSITION

§32 A noun in apposition normally agrees with the noun it defines in case, though not necessarily in gender and number.

(i) Normal apposition of the type: **ста́рший инжене́р Ивано́в (Ива-** **но́ва,** see note [1] to §20), **ру́сский компози́тор Гли́нка, сёстры** **Фёдоровы, го́род Оде́сса** (*the city* of *Odessa*):

Мы говори́ли **со ста́ршим инжене́ром Ивано́вым (Ивано́вой)**.

Мы ви́дели о́перу «Ива́н Суса́нин» **ру́сского компози́тора** **Гли́нки**.

Мы слу́шали конце́рт **сестёр Фёдоровых**.

Я жил тогда́ **в черномо́рском го́роде Оде́ссе**.

Also:

Мы бы́ли в Ленингра́де, бы́вшем Санкт-Петербу́рге, знамени́-той столи́це Росси́йской Импе́рии.

We were in Leningrad, the former St Petersburg, the famous capital of the Russian Empire.

(ii) There is no agreement in the case of names of lakes, islands, mountains, railway stations:

на о́зере Байка́л на о́строве Сума́тра

на горе́ Эльбру́с на ста́нции «Новокузне́цкая»

Many foreign place-names, and Russian place-names ending in **-ово** and **-ино** are considered indeclinable:

в го́роде О́сло в Де́ли из села́ Ива́ново

(iii) Appositions with *as*:

Я вспомина́ю об э́том дне, как о са́мом счастли́вом в мое́й жи́зни.

I remember this day as the happiest in my life.

See also §173.

§33 Titles of books, plays, novels, names of hotels, cinemas, ships, etc. are put in inverted commas. When standing in apposition to a preceding noun, they are indeclinable, being 'protected' as it were by that noun. Compare:

Я э́то чита́л в газе́те «Пра́вда».   Я э́то чита́л в «Пра́вде».

Я ви́дел о́перу «Бори́с Годуно́в».   Я ви́дел «Бори́са Годуно́ва».

Я останови́лся в гости́нице «Москва́».   Я останови́лся в «Москве́».

Мы е́хали на теплохо́де «Ба́лтика».   Мы е́хали на «Ба́лтике».

§34 In hyphenated nouns of the type **го́род-краса́вец, Москва́-река́, студе́нт-второку́рсник**, both words are declined:

Они́ плы́ли по Москве́-реке́.

They were sailing down the River Moskva.

Я зна́ю э́того студе́нта-второку́рсника.

I know this second-year student.

жи́тели го́рода-краса́вца Ленингра́да

the inhabitants of the beautiful city of Leningrad

The Adjective

THE LONG AND SHORT FORMS OF ADJECTIVES

I. AS COMPLEMENT OF быть

§35 The long form can be used both attributively and predicatively. The short form can only be used predicatively:

Это трýдный перевóд.	*This is a difficult translation.*
Перевóд трýден, перевóд трýдный.	*The translation is difficult.*

§36 The short form is used in bold assertions and broad generalisations; it is more typical of written than of spoken Russian:

Все велúкие úстины прóсты.	*All great truths are simple.*
Úмя Пýшкина бессмéртно.	*The name of Pushkin is immortal.*
Ты óчень неблагодáрен.	*You are very ungrateful.*
Земля великá и прекрáсна.	*The earth is great and beautiful.*
Вóздух был чист и ясен.	*The air was pure and fresh.*

§37 The short form is used in the complement of **быть** with such adjectives as **виновáт**, *guilty*; **готóв**, *ready*; **жив**, *alive*; **прав**, *right*:

Вы готóвы?	*Are you ready?*
Он был прав.	*He was right.*
Он жив и здорóв.	*He is alive and well.*

Рад exists only in the short form:

Я был рад вúдеть егó.	*I was glad to see him.*

The short form is also used with expressions of courtesy: Бýдьте добры́, бýдьте так любéзны, *be so kind*; бýдьте здорóвы (when saying good-bye); and with the imperative generally: Будь спокóен! *Be calm* (i.e. *don't worry*).

It is also used with **слúшком**, *too* (*much*, etc.), or when it is understood:

Эти тýфли малы́.	*These shoes are too small.*

The short form is normally used when the adjective is followed by an extension:

Э́тот учени́к си́лен в матема́тике.	*This pupil is good at mathematics.*
Он похо́ж на отца́.	*He is like his father.*
Он был дово́лен жи́знью.	*He was pleased with life.*
Я был бли́зок к и́стине.	*I was near the truth.*

When the adjective is qualified by **так, (не)доста́точно**, etc.:

В мое́й голове́ родило́сь подозре́ние, что слепо́й не так слеп, как мне ка́жется. [Ле́рмонтов]

In my mind there dawned (lit. *was born*) *the suspicion that the blind boy was not as blind as I thought.*

See §41.

§38 The long form of the adjective is used in the predicate to express fundamental characteristics, but the resulting statement is less categorical than it would be with the corresponding short form:

Она́ хоро́шая, до́брая, сла́вная. Я её о́чень люблю́. [Че́хов]	
She is good, kind and wonderful. I love her very much.	
Како́й он у́мный!	*How clever he is!*
Он глу́пый.	*He is a silly man.*

but:

Он глуп.	*He is stupid, a fool* (see §36).

§39 Relative adjectives have no short form. These are adjectives which:

(i) Refer to materials: **деревя́нный**, *wooden*; **ка́менный**, *made of stone*; **золото́й**, *golden*.

(ii) Denote geographical origin: **ру́сский**, *Russian*; **англи́йский**, *English*; thus, too, all other adjectives ending in **-ский**, e.g. **полити́ческий**, *political*; **дру́жеский**, *friendly*[1]; and **иностра́нный**, *foreign*; **родно́й**, *native*.

(iii) Indicate relative position in a series: **пе́рвый**, *first*, and all ordinal numerals; **сре́дний**, *middle, average*; **после́дний**, *last*; **остально́й**, *remaining*.

---

[1] Adverbs end in **-ски**: **по-ру́сски**, *in Russian*; **полити́чески**, *politically*.

(iv) Refer to time: **вечéрний**, *evening*; **лéтний**, *summer's*; **ежемé-сячный**, *monthly*; **вчерáшний**, *yesterday's*.

They include, in fact, all adjectives ending in -**ний** (except **сúний**, *blue*, and **úскренний**, *sincere*): **соcéдний**, *neighbouring*; **вéрхний**, *upper*; **здéшний**, *local*; etc.

Все домá бы́ли кáменные.
All the houses were made of stone.

Э́тот самолёт не совéтский, а америкáнский.
This aircraft is not Soviet, but American.

Кто послéдний?
Who is last (in the queue)?

Э́та газéта не сегóдняшняя, а вчерáшняя.
This is not today's paper, but yesterday's.

The short form of **большóй** is **велúк**, of **мáленький**, **мал**.

All diminutives ending in -**енький** lose that ending in the short form. Thus, **онá óчень хорошá** means *she is very pretty* (short form of **хорóшенькая**); **онá óчень хорóшая**, *she is a very good person.*

§40 In the spoken language, the long form is used in the predicate with increasing frequency:

Их дом мáленький, но уютный.
Their house is small but comfortable.

У неё сéрдце óчень дóброе.
She has a very kind heart.

Сотрýдники библиотéки óчень любéзные.
The librarians are very helpful.

Домá в гóроде бы́ли нóвые.
The houses in town were new.

Плáтье на ней стáрое.
The dress she is wearing is old.

See also §42.

§41 If the adjective is preceded by *so, as, such a, what, which, how,* **такóй**, **какóй** are used with the long form and **так**, **как** with the short form:

Пьéса былá такáя интерéсная. (Пьéса былá так интерéсна.)
The play was so interesting.

Я давно́ не ви́дел тако́й интере́сной пье́сы, как э́та (see §173).
I have not seen as interesting a play as this one for a long time.

Како́й он стра́нный.   *What an odd person he is.*

Как он стра́нен (сего́дня).   *How odd he is (today).*
See also §§36, 38.

§42 Often an adjective that is in effect attributive is separated from its noun:

Утро бы́ло ти́хое, тёплое.   *It was a quiet, warm morning.*

У меня́ рабо́та спе́шная.   *I have some urgent work to do.*

Глаза́ у неё се́рые.   *She has grey eyes.*

§43 Adjectives in apposition are always in the long form:

Ве́рный своему́ обеща́нию, он появи́лся на друго́е у́тро.
True to his word, he turned up on the following morning.

Он шёл по доро́ге, бо́дрый и весёлый.[1]
He walked along the road, bright and cheerful.

§44 With the past and future of **быть**, the instrumental of the long form is in spoken Russian used rather less frequently than the nominative (long or short form). The instrumental is relatively rarely used to describe persons as they appeared on a particular occasion:

Наде́юсь, что представле́ние бы́ло (бу́дет) уда́чно/е (уда́чным).
I hope the performance was (will be) successful.

Их встре́ча была́ серде́чна/я и прия́тна/я (серде́чной и прия́тной).

Their encounter was cordial and pleasant.
Contrast:

Когда́ он был ма́леньким, ...
When he was small ...
with:

На ве́чере он был ве́жлив и сде́ржан.
At the party he was polite and reserved.

The instrumental is, however, used regularly with the infinitive and gerund:

На́до быть внима́тельным.
You have to be attentive.

[1] The short form, **он ... бодр и ве́сел**, would constitute a predicate: *he ... is bright and cheerful*; cf. §106.

36

Бу́дучи не о́чень тала́нтливым, он не мог спра́виться с э́той
тру́дной зада́чей.
Being not very talented he could not cope with this difficult task.

II. WITH OTHER LINK VERBS

§45 The instrumental is used regularly with **станови́ться/стать,
де́латься/с-, каза́ться/по-, ока́зываться/оказа́ться**, etc.:

Жизнь ста́ла тяжёлой, почти́ несно́сной.
Life became hard, almost unbearable.

Пье́са каза́лась о́чень интере́сной.
The play seemed to be very interesting.

Он оказа́лся тяжело́ больны́м.
He was (lit. proved to be) seriously ill.

Он притворя́лся спя́щим.
He pretended to be asleep.

Note also the use of the instrumental in complements of the direct
object:

Э́то сде́лало его́ о́чень счастли́вым.
This made him very happy.

Я не нахожу́ э́ту кни́гу интере́сной.
I do not find this book interesting.

The short form is found in certain expressions:

e.g. Он оста́лся дово́лен их рабо́той.
He was pleased with their work.

POSSESSIVE ADJECTIVES

§46 **Мой (моя́, моё, мой); твой (твоя́,** etc.**); наш (на́ша, на́ше,
на́ши); ваш (ва́ша,** etc.**); его́, её, их** (*indecl.*):

Э́то моя́ кни́га.	*This is my book.*
Его́ сестра́ — студе́нтка.	*His sister is a student.*
Их дом за́ городом.	*Their house is in the country.*
Он взял мою́ кни́гу.	*He took my book.*
Я взял его́ кни́гу.	*I took his book.*

В на́шей (его́, её, их) кварти́ре четы́ре больши́х ко́мнаты.
In our (his, her, their) flat there are four large rooms.

§47 Свой (своя́, своё, свои́) is used with all three persons, singular and plural, and agrees with its noun, like **мой, твой**, etc. It refers to the subject in a simple sentence, and to the subject *of its clause* in a complex sentence:

Я чита́ю свою́ кни́гу.	*I am reading my book.*
Он чита́ет свою́ кни́гу.	*He is reading his book.*
Мы чита́ем свою́ кни́гу.	*We are reading our book.*

NOTE: **Он чита́ет его́ кни́гу** means *A is reading B's book.*

Compare:

Он впервы́е встре́тил **свою́** жену́ на балу́.
He had first met his wife at a dance.

Он говори́т, что **его́** жена́ танцу́ет прекра́сно.
He says that his wife dances beautifully.

Он о́чень дово́лен **свое́й** но́вой рабо́той.
He is very pleased with his new job.

Он говори́т, что **его́** но́вая рабо́та о́чень интере́сна.
He says that his new job is very interesting.

Ива́н Петро́вич и **его́** жена́[1] (с жено́й) е́хали в о́тпуск.
Ivan Petrovich and his wife were going on holiday.

Свой is not used in the nominative except with **у меня́**, etc. and certain idiomatic expressions:

У него́ свой дом.	*He has a house of his own.*
Мы здесь свои́ лю́ди.	*We are amongst friends.*
Своя́ руба́шка бли́же к те́лу.	*Charity begins at home.*

NOTE I

Нью-Йо́рк с **его́** огро́мными небоскрёбами произво́дит незабыва́емое впечатле́ние на ка́ждого прие́зжего.
New York, with its huge skyscrapers, makes an unforgettable impression on the visitor.

С его́ огро́мными небоскрёбами is not an integral part of the predicate, but an extension of the subject.

Contrast:

Свои́ми огро́мными небоскрёбами Нью-Йо́рк произво́дит незабыва́емое впечатле́ние на ка́ждого прие́зжего.
With its huge skyscrapers, New York makes an unforgettable impression on the visitor.

[1] **И его́ жена́** is an extension of the subject; see Note 1, below.

Here **своими огромными небоскрёбами** are the means whereby the impression is created. Cf. §24(i).

NOTE 2

It is strictly more correct to say that **свой** and **себя** (see §78, i) refer to the person performing the action, since this is not always the subject:

Пассажир попросил носильщика отнести **его** багаж к выходу.
The traveller asked the porter to take his luggage to the exit.

Свой багаж would mean *the porter's own luggage.*

§48 (i) The possessive adjective is usually omitted:

(*a*) With relationships:

Он любит (свою) мать.
He loves his mother.

(*b*) Where possession is not emphasised:

Я открыл книгу и начал читать.
I opened my book and began to read.

Он надел пальто и вышел.
He put on his coat and went out.

Contrast:

По ошибке она надела не свою, а сестрину шляпу.
By mistake she did not put on her own hat, but her sister's.

(*c*) With parts of the body where it is almost always omitted:

Она покачала головой.   *She shook her head.*

Он пошёл мыть руки.   *He went to wash his hands.*

The construction with the dative is more idiomatic:

Он сломал себе ногу.   *He broke his leg.*

Нечаянно кто-то наступил   *Somebody accidentally stepped*
ему на ногу.   *on his foot.*

Она пожала мне руку.   *She shook hands with me.*

(ii) The possessive adjective may be rendered by **у меня, у себя**, etc.:

У меня в комнате стоит большой письменный стол.
In my room there is a large desk.

Я (он) занимался у себя в комнате.
I (he) was studying in my (his) room.

Он пошёл к себе в комнату.   *He went to his room.*

Он вошёл ко мне в комнату.   *He came to my room.*

For further uses of **себя**, see §78(i).

THE COMPARATIVE AND SUPERLATIVE OF ADJECTIVES

NOTE. A distinction must be made between attributive and predicative adjectives.

THE COMPARATIVE

§49 The comparative of PREDICATIVE adjectives (and adverbs) is regularly formed by the addition of -ee, e.g. краси́в, -а, -о, -ы — краси́вее; when the comparative stem differs from that of the positive, -e is added to the stem, e.g. бога́т — бога́че, широ́к — ши́ре. This comparative is indeclinable:

Э́то тру́дно.	*This is difficult.*
Э́то трудне́е.	*This is more difficult.*
Он умён.	*He is clever.*
Он умне́е её (see §52).	*He is cleverer than she.*
Э́то сто́ит о́чень до́рого.	*This is very dear.*
Э́то сто́ит гора́здо доро́же (see §53).	*This is much dearer.*

§50 The comparative of ATTRIBUTIVE adjectives consists of the indeclinable **бо́лее** and the long form of the adjective[1]:

Э́то му́дрый челове́к.	*This is a wise person.*
Он бо́лее му́дрый челове́к.	*He is a wiser man.*
Они́ жи́ли в но́вом до́ме.	*They lived in a new house.*
Мы жи́ли в бо́лее но́вом до́ме, чем они́ (see §52).	*We lived in a newer house than they.*

§51 There are eight adjectives (four pairs of opposites) which form their attributive comparatives without **бо́лее**:

	Positive	Attributive Comparative	Predicative Comparative (and adverb)
good	хоро́ший	лу́чший	лу́чше
bad	плохо́й	ху́дший	ху́же

[1] However, the short form can be used in an attributive sense when immediately following its noun:

Он получи́л ко́мнату бо́льше мое́й.
He was given a room (which was) bigger than mine.

40

	Positive	Attributive Comparative	Predicative Comparative (and adverb)
big	большо́й	бо́льший	бо́льше[1]
small	ма́ленький	ме́ньший	ме́ньше[1]
old	ста́рый	ста́рший[2]	ста́рший
young	молодо́й	мла́дший[2]	моло́же
tall, high	высо́кий	вы́сший	вы́ше
low	ни́зкий	ни́зший	ни́же

The declined comparatives (лу́чший, etc.) can also have superlative force; see §55(i).

§52 *Than* is normally translated by the genitive of comparison:

Наш дом бо́льше ва́шего.	*Our house is bigger than yours.*
Он ста́рше меня́.	*He is older than I.*
Ра́ньше обы́чного.	*Earlier than usual.*

Чем is used with the compound comparative (formed with **бо́лее**). Compare:

Ру́сский язы́к трудне́е францу́зского.
Ру́сский бо́лее тру́дный язы́к, чем францу́зский.
Russian is harder than French.

Чем is also used where the genitive of comparison would be ambiguous.
Compare:

Я зна́ю Ива́на лу́чше, чем Со́ню.
I know Ivan better than (I know) Sonya.
Я зна́ю Ива́на лу́чше, чем Со́ня.
I know Ivan better than Sonya (does).

Where cases other than the nominative and accusative (particularly with prepositions) are involved, the genitive cannot be used:

Я говори́л с ней ча́ще, чем с её бра́том.
I spoke to her more often than to her brother.

[1] Бо́льше is also the comparative of мно́го, *much, many* and ме́ньше of ма́ло, *little, few.*
[2] ста́рший, мла́дший as adjectives mean *senior, junior:* ста́рший (мла́дший) лейтена́нт, *senior (junior) lieutenant.*

§53 **По-** used as a prefix before an indeclinable comparative restricts the meaning: **погро́мче**, *a little louder*; **поста́рше**, *a little older*. *Much* with the comparative is **гора́здо**, not **мно́го**:

> Она́ гора́здо ста́рше меня́.   *She is much older than I.*

Even (still) older is **ещё ста́рше**; see §171.

Note:

как мо́жно скоре́е	*as soon as possible*
Иди́те скоре́е!	*Come quickly!*
всё ху́же	*worse and worse*
Ти́ше!	*Quiet!*

For expressions of difference and multiples (*two years older, twice as old*), see §70.

THE SUPERLATIVE

§54 The superlative is formed with **са́мый** and the long form of the adjective. This form is used both attributively and predicatively. The predicative superlative can also be expressed by **бо́льше всего́** or **бо́льше всех** and other comparatives followed by **всего́** or **всех**. Compare:

> Э́то са́мая интере́сная кни́га, каку́ю я когда́-либо чита́л.
> *This is the most interesting book I have ever read.*
> Э́та кни́га са́мая интере́сная, каку́ю я когда́-либо чита́л.
> *This book is the most interesting one that I have ever read.*
> Он бо́льше всего́ люби́л му́зыку.
> *He liked music best of all (better than anything else).*
> Му́зыку он люби́л бо́льше всех.
> *He liked music better than anybody else (did).*

§55 (i) With the eight adjectives listed in §51 (хоро́ший, плохо́й, etc.) the superlative can be formed with **са́мый** followed by either the positive or the comparative.

Лу́чший, etc. can be used by themselves in a superlative sense:

> Attributive: Вот молодо́й студе́нт.
> Вот мла́дший студе́нт (comparative).
> Вот са́мый молодо́й (са́мый мла́дший, мла́дший) студе́нт (superlative).

Predicative: Он мо́лод, он молодо́й (see §§35, 40).

Он моло́же (comparative).

Он са́мый молодо́й (са́мый мла́дший, мла́дший, моло́же всех) (superlative).

(ii) The superlatives in **-ейший, -айший** are generally confined to the written language, e.g.

Велича́йший ру́сский поэ́т Пу́шкин.

Pushkin, Russia's greatest poet.

О́ксфорд — старе́йший университе́т А́нглии.

Oxford is the oldest university in England.

They are, however, commonly used without a literally superlative meaning, e.g. **у него́ умне́йшая** (= о́чень у́мная) **жена́; э́то важне́йший** (= о́чень ва́жный) **вопро́с; в ближа́йшее время** (= о́чень ско́ро).

Э́то не име́ет ни мале́йшего значе́ния.

This does not make the slightest difference.

Superlatives formed with **наи-** also have a literary or scientific flavour. They indicate absolute superiority etc., e.g. **наилу́чший результа́т**, *the very best result*, and **наибо́льшие достиже́ния**, *the greatest achievements.*

Note also **наибо́лее**, *most*, and **наиме́нее**, *least*:

наибо́лее сло́жный вопро́с	*the most complex issue*
наиме́нее уда́чный спо́соб рабо́ты	*the least successful method of working*

Numerals

§56 (i) **Оди́н** (**одна́, одно́, одни́**) functions like an attributive adjective and agrees with its noun in number, gender and case:

в оди́н прекра́сный день   *one fine day*

Вся семья́ жила́ в одно́й ма́ленькой ко́мнате.
The whole family lived in one small room.

Они́ не по́няли ни одного́ сло́ва.
They did not understand a single word.

This agreement also applies to compound numerals whose last unit is 'one' (NOT 'eleven', see below, §59):

В го́роде постро́ен сто со́рок оди́н но́вый дом.
One hundred and forty-one new houses have been built in the town.

(ii) **Оди́н** may render the indefinite article:

Вчера́ я встре́тил одного́ челове́ка, кото́рого я знал давно́.
Yesterday I met a person whom I had known long ago.

See also §§14, 81.

(iii) **Оди́н** can mean *the same* with or without **и тот же**:

Мы жи́ли с ним в одно́м (и том же) до́ме.
We lived in the same house.

See also §77.

(iv) It means *only, nothing but*, as in:

Он был в одно́й руба́шке.   *He was in his shirt-sleeves.*

Одна́ забо́та мне с тобо́й.   *I have nothing but trouble with you.*

(v) When used in apposition to a noun or pronoun, **оди́н** means *alone, on his own*, etc.:

Он оста́лся в до́ме оди́н.   *He stayed in the house on his own.*

Ему́ надое́ло остава́ться в до́ме одному́.   *He became tired of staying in the house on his own.*

(vi) **Одни́** (*pl.*) is used:

(*a*) With nouns existing in the plural only:

Одни́ но́жницы, одни́ су́тки, одни́ са́ни.
One pair of scissors, one day (twenty-four hours), a sledge.

(*b*) As an indefinite pronoun, *some*:

Одни́ игра́ли в ка́рты, одни́ (or други́е) ти́хо разгова́ривали.
Some were playing cards, others talking quietly.

See also §81.

(*c*) Meaning *only*:

В на́шей шко́ле одни́ (or то́лько) ма́льчики.
There are only boys at our school.

§57 DECLENSIONS OF CARDINAL NUMERALS

(i)	*nom.*	два, две (*f.*)[1]	три	четы́ре
	acc.	like nominative or genitive[2]		
	gen.	двух	трёх	четырёх
	dat.	двум	трём	четырём
	instr.	двумя́	тремя́	четырьмя́
	prep.	о двух	о трёх	о четырёх

(ii) **Пять** and all other numerals ending in -ь decline like feminine nouns of the type **ночь**:

nom., acc.	пять	во́семь	
gen.	пяти́	восьми́	
dat.	пяти́	восьми́	
instr.	пятью́	восемью́ (восьмью́)	
prep.	о пяти́	о восьми́	

nom., acc.	три́дцать англи́йских студе́нтов
gen.	тридцати́ англи́йских студе́нтов
dat.	тридцати́ англи́йским студе́нтам
instr.	тридцатью́ англи́йскими студе́нтами
prep.	о тридцати́ англи́йских студе́нтах

[1] **Оба, о́бе,** *both,* has a separate feminine form throughout: *nom., acc.* о́ба, о́бе; *acc., gen.* обо́их, обе́их; *dat.* обо́им, обе́им; *instr.* обо́ими, обе́ими; *prep.* об обо́их, обе́их.

[2] See §21.

45

(iii) The numbers 40, 90 and 100 have two forms only: **со́рок, девяно́сто, сто** (*nom., acc.*) and **сорока́, девяно́ста, ста** (all other cases):

со́рок но́вых домо́в   *forty new houses*
бо́лее сорока́ но́вых домо́в   *more than forty new houses*
в сорока́ но́вых дома́х   *in forty new houses*

(iv) With **пятьдеся́т** (50), **шестьдеся́т** (60), **се́мьдесят** (70), **во́семьдесят** (80), both halves of the compound are declined, the latter as though ending in -**ь**:

nom., acc.	пятьдеся́т домо́в
gen.	пяти́десяти домо́в
dat.	пяти́десяти дома́м
instr.	пятью́десятью дома́ми
prep.	в пяти́десяти дома́х

(v) **Две́сти** (200), **три́ста** (300), **четы́реста** (400) and **пятьсо́т** (500) decline as follows:

nom.	две́сти	три́ста	пятьсо́т
acc.	две́сти	три́ста	пятьсо́т
gen.	двухсо́т	трёхсо́т	пятисо́т
dat.	двумста́м	трёмста́м	пятиста́м
instr.	двумяста́ми	тремяста́ми	пятьюста́ми
prep.	о двухста́х	о трёхста́х	о пятиста́х

-**ста** (-**сти**) may be regarded as a neuter plural noun (cf. **места́**): -**ста**, -**сот**, -**стам**, -**стами**, -**стах**, e.g.

две́сти (три́ста, пятьсо́т) но́вых домо́в
two hundred (three hundred, five hundred) new houses
бо́лее двухсо́т (трёхсо́т, пятисо́т) но́вых домо́в
more than two hundred (three hundred, five hundred) new houses
в двухста́х (трёхста́х, пятиста́х) но́вых дома́х
in two hundred (three hundred, five hundred) new houses

(vi) **Ты́сяча** (1000) and **миллио́н** (*million*) are both nouns and are followed by the genitive plural:

две ты́сячи но́вых домо́в   *two thousand new houses*
бо́лее двух ты́сяч но́вых домо́в *more than two thousand new houses*

пять миллио́нов но́вых домо́в *five million new houses*

в пяти́ миллио́нах но́вых домо́в *in five million new houses*

NOUNS AND ADJECTIVES AFTER NUMERALS

§58 AFTER 2, 3, 4; 22, 23, 24, ETC.

Два (*m.* and *n.*), две (*f.*), три, четы́ре, are followed by a noun in the GENITIVE SINGULAR:

> два (три, четы́ре) бра́та, окна́

> две (три, четы́ре) де́вушки, кни́ги

> 22 (два́дцать два) ученика́

> 343 (три́ста со́рок три) кни́ги, ученика́ и т. д.

The adjective is in the GENITIVE PLURAL (with feminine nouns it is usually in the *nom.pl.*):

це́лых два часа́	*two whole hours*
два молоды́х англича́нина	*two young Englishmen*
три ру́сских (ру́сские) кни́ги	*three Russian books*

This rule applies when the whole phrase is, as it were, in the nominative (or nominative and accusative in the case of inanimate nouns). For other cases, see §60 (i).

Вчера́ четы́ре сове́тских инжене́ра посети́ли наш заво́д.
Four Soviet engineers visited our factory yesterday.

Вчера́ ве́чером я прочита́л два ру́сских расска́за.
I read two Russian stories last night.

§59 After the following numbers: 5-20; 25-30; 35-40, 50, etc.; 100, 200, etc. and all compound numerals, except those listed in §§56 and 58, *both* the adjective and the noun are in the GENITIVE PLURAL:

> 5 (пять) ру́сских уче́бников

> 12 (двена́дцать) молоды́х англича́н

> 569 (пятьсо́т шестьдеся́т де́вять) англи́йских шко́льников

§60 (i) After numerals in oblique cases.

In the genitive, dative, instrumental and prepositional, the constructions described in paragraphs 58 and 59 are NOT used. Instead, the numeral agrees in case with its adjective and noun; the latter are in their respective case in the plural: в два часа́, but о́коло двух часо́в, к двум часа́м, двумя́ часа́ми, etc. See also §57.

три но́вых до́ма	*three new houses*
в трёх но́вых дома́х	*in three new houses*

Вчера́ два англи́йских учи́теля (две англи́йские учи́тельницы) посети́ли на́шу шко́лу.
Two English school-teachers visited our school yesterday.

Мы встре́тили двух англи́йских учителе́й (учи́тельниц).
We met two English school-teachers.

Мы говори́ли с двумя́ англи́йскими учителя́ми (учи́тельни-цами).
We were talking to two English school-teachers.

NOTE. The animate accusative (genitive form) is only used of два/ две, три, четы́ре (NOT of compound numerals ending in 2, 3, 4, nor 5-20, etc.):

Мы встре́тили два́дцать два англи́йских учи́теля (два́дцать две англи́йских учи́тельницы).
We met twenty-two English school-teachers.

Мы встре́тили пять англи́йских учителе́й (учи́тельниц).
We met five English school-teachers.

(ii) The treatment of words of quantity (мно́го, немно́го, ма́ло, ско́лько, не́сколько, etc.) is similar to that of numerals. In the nominative (and accusative) they are followed by a noun in the genitive singular or plural (e.g. мно́го рабо́ты, *much work*; мно́го люде́й, *many people*). The adjective always agrees with its noun in gender, case and NUMBER: мно́го интере́сной рабо́ты, мно́го интере́сных люде́й. (Contrast §58.)

Мно́го and similar words decline in the plural like adjectives: мно́го/ мно́гие, мно́гих, мно́гим, мно́гими, о мно́гих:

У мно́гих (ско́льких, немно́гих, не́скольких) люде́й...
Many (how many, a few) people have...

со мно́гими (со ско́лькими, с немно́гими, с не́сколькими) людьми́
with many (how many, a few) people

во мно́гих (во ско́льких и т. д.) слу́чаях
in many (how many, etc.) cases

Мно́гое and мно́гие are used as nouns (*many things, many people*)[1]:

---

[1] There is a stylistic difference between мно́гие лю́ди and мно́го люде́й and between мно́гие го́ды and мно́го лет, the second alternative being the more usual form.

На́до бу́дет обсужда́ть мно́гое.	*Many things will have to be discussed.*
Он мно́гим недово́лен.	*There is much (are many things) he is dissatisfied with.*
Во мно́гом он прав.	*He is right in many ways.*
Мно́гие так ду́мают.	*Many people think so.*
Для мно́гих э́то бы́ло непоня́тно.	*This was incomprehensible to many people.*

Similarly, **ско́лько,** *how much, how many;* **не́сколько, немно́го,** *a little, a few;* **ма́ло,** *little, few:*

Ско́лько вре́мени? Мно́го (не́сколько, немно́го, ма́ло) вре́мени.
How much time? Much (a little, little) time.

Ско́лько люде́й? Мно́го (не́сколько, немно́го, ма́ло) люде́й.
How many people? Many (a few, few) people.

в не́скольких слова́х	*in a few words*
за немно́гими исключе́ниями	*with few exceptions*

NOTE. **Ма́ло** indicates a very small quantity or number, while **немно́го** can indicate a certain, if limited, quantity or number. Compare:

Он ма́ло рабо́тал.	*He did very little work.*

and:

Он немно́го рабо́тал.	*He did some (a little) work.*

Note also:

Учёных мно́го, у́мных ма́ло.	*There are many learned people, but few intelligent ones.*

§61 FRACTIONS

a half ($\frac{1}{2}$) **полови́на** (+ *gen.*); note also:

half an hour	полчаса́
a good half hour	до́брые (до́брых) полчаса́

one and a half ($1\frac{1}{2}$) **полтора́** (*f.* **полторы́**) (+ *gen. sing.*):

one and a half hours	полтора́ часа́

two and a half, three and a half, hours **два с полови́ной часа́, три с полови́ной часа́**

one-fifth, two-fifths ($\frac{1}{5}$, $\frac{2}{5}$) **одна́ пя́тая** (**часть,** *part,* being understood), **две пя́тых** (**ча́сти**)

a third, a quarter ($\frac{1}{3}$, $\frac{1}{4}$) **однá треть, однá чéтверть** +*gen. sing.*

two-thirds, three-quarters ($\frac{2}{3}$, $\frac{3}{4}$) **две трéти (трéтьих), три чéтверти
(четвёртых)** +*gen. sing.*

§62 An approximate number is expressed by inversion of numeral
and noun:

Онú ждáли часá три (óколо трёх часóв).	*They waited for about three hours.*
Мы éдем дней на пять.[1]	*We are going for about five days.*
лет чéрез двáдцать[1]	*some twenty years later*
мужчúна лет сорокá	*a man of about forty*

With a single unit, **с** (+ *acc.*) is used:

С минýту онú простоя́ли мóлча.	*For about a minute they stood in silence.*
Мы прóбыли там с недéлю.	*We stayed there for about a week.*

§63 COLLECTIVES

Двóе, трóе, чéтверо, etc. are used when a given number of persons
is expressed as a group rather than as so many individuals:

(i) With masculine nouns indicating human beings:

Все чéтверо вошлú в дом.	*All four of them entered the house.*
Онú втроём пошлú.	*The three of them went off.*
Мы нашлú всех троúх.	*We found all three of them.*

With **дéти**:

У них двóе детéй.	*They have two children.*

and nouns in **-ёнок**:

Волк и сéмеро козля́т.	*The wolf and the seven kids.*

(ii) With **нас, вас, их**:

Нас бы́ло чéтверо.	*There were four of us.*
Их бы́ло пя́теро.	*There were five of them.*

They are also used with nouns existing in the plural only:

двóе нóжниц, *two pairs of scissors*   **трóе сýток,** *three days*

---

[1] Note the position of the preposition.

50

but:

бо́лее трёх (rather than тройх) сýток   *more than three days*

§64 DISTRIBUTIVES

One each is translated by **по** + *dat.*:

Учи́тель ро́здал ученика́м по (одно́й) кни́ге, по (одному́) учéбнику.

The teacher handed the pupils a book (a textbook) each.

With other numerals, **по** + *acc.* is normally used:

по́ две кни́ги, по́ два учéбника   *two books (textbooks) each*

по пять книг   *five books each*

по два́дцать (по сто) рублéй   *twenty (one hundred) roubles each*

The use of the dative with numerals from 5 to 20, etc. (по пяти́ книг) is found, but is not common in everyday Russian.

§65 THE VERB AFTER NUMERALS

(i) **Оди́н** and compounds ending in **оди́н** have a singular verb (agreeing in gender, in the past tense):

На собра́ние при́был пятьдеся́т оди́н делега́т.

Fifty-one delegates attended the conference.

(ii) With other numerals both the neuter singular and plural are used. The following may serve as a guide.

The PLURAL verb is used :

(*a*) With **два/две, три, четы́ре, дво́е, тро́е, чéтверо** (but see §63, ii), etc.:

Два това́рища шли по́ лесу.

Two men were walking through a forest.

Пя́теро шли по у́лице.

Five men were walking on the road.

Откры́ты две но́вых чита́льни.

Two new reading-rooms have been opened.

На столé лежа́т три но́вых журна́ла.

There are three new periodicals on the table.

(*b*) With compound numerals ending in 2, 3, 4:

Со́рок четы́ре человéка поéхали в Совéтский Сою́з.

Forty-four persons went to the Soviet Union.

51

(c) When the numeral is preceded by **все, э́ти**:

Все пять ма́льчиков сиде́ли вокру́г костра́.
All the five boys were sitting around the bonfire.
Э́ти семь книг ку́плены неда́вно.
These seven books were bought recently.

(d) When identical actions are clearly performed separately:

Пять ма́льчиков разбежа́лись в ра́зные сто́роны.
The five boys ran off in various directions.

(iii) The NEUTER SINGULAR verb is normal:

(a) With expressions of time:

Прошло́ три го́да (де́сять лет).	*Three (ten) years went by.*
Прошло́ полго́да.	*Six months went by.*

(b) When the verb expresses position rather than movement:

В ко́мнате находи́лось два́дцать пять челове́к.
There were twenty-five persons in the room.

(c) With approximate number:

В кла́ссе бы́ло ученико́в три́дцать (о́коло тридцати́ ученико́в).
There were about thirty pupils in the class.

В кла́ссе бы́ло пять и́ли шесть но́вых ученико́в.
There were five or six new pupils in the class.

(d) When the numeral is preceded by **всего́, то́лько**:

На экску́рсию пошло́ всего́ пятна́дцать челове́к.
Only fifteen persons went on the excursion.

(e) With expressions of quantity (**мно́го, ма́ло, не́сколько, большинство́**, etc.):

Мно́го люде́й гуля́ло по на́бережной.
Many people were walking along the promenade.

На столе́ лежи́т не́сколько но́вых журна́лов.
There are several new periodicals on the table.

Большинство́ голосова́ло за предложе́ние.
The majority voted for the motion.

When, however, the subject and verb are separated by other elements in the sentence, the grammatical connexion is lost sight of and a plural verb is often used. There is a further tendency to use a plural verb with animate subjects and the singular with inanimate ones:

Большинство людей в зале слушали(-о) оратора внимательно.
Most people in the hall listened to the speaker attentively.

Несколько новых книг лежало на столе.
Several new books were lying on the table.

The singular is found when the verb precedes the word of quantity:

В комнату вошло несколько человек.
Several persons entered the room.

§66 ORDINALS

These are normal attributive adjectives (but see §39); see under Dates (§67) below.

§67 DATES

Dates are expressed by ordinal numbers in the neuter nominative or genitive, **число** being understood:

Какое сегодня число?
What is the date today?

Сегодня первое (второе, двадцать пятое) мая.
Today is the 1st (2nd, 25th) of May.

Какого числа вы выехали из Лондона?
On what date did you leave London?

Мы выехали из Лондона десятого июля.
We left London on the 10th of July.

Сегодня понедельник, третье декабря, тысяча девятьсот шестидесятого года.
Today is Monday, the 3rd of December, 1960.

В понедельник, третьего декабря тысяча девятьсот шестидесятого года.
On Monday, the 3rd of December, 1960.

At the top of letters it is usual to write the date in the genitive:

3-го мая, 1960 г.   (3 мая 1960)

In 1960 (without specific date) is:

в тысяча девятьсот шестидесятом году.

§68 AGE

The person (building, etc.) is in the dative:

Сколько вам лет?
How old are you?

Мне шестна́дцать лет (два́дцать оди́н год).
I am sixteen (twenty-one).

Э́тому зда́нию бо́лее двухсо́т лет.
This building is over two hundred years old.

На про́шлой неде́ле мне испо́лнилось шестна́дцать лет.
I was sixteen last week.

Ему́ идёт шестна́дцатый год.
He is in his sixteenth year.

двадцати́ пяти́ лет, в два́дцать пять лет (о́троду)
at the age of twenty-five

на пятидеся́том году́ о́троду
in his fiftieth year

§69 (i) USE OF год

Год is used with **оди́н** and compound numbers ending in **оди́н**:

оди́н год   два́дцать оди́н год

Note the *prep. sing.* as in **в э́том году́.**

Го́да (*gen. sing.*) is used with 2, 3 and 4 and compound numbers ending in 2, 3 and 4:

два (три, четы́ре) го́да, два́дцать два (два́дцать три, два́дцать четы́ре) го́да

Лет (*gen.pl.*) is used with numerals from 5 to 20 and other numerals not included above, and with words of quantity:

пять (шесть, два́дцать) лет, сто лет, пятьсо́т лет; мно́го лет

and generally as the genitive plural of **год**:

го́ды войны́	*the war years*
собы́тия вое́нных лет	*the events of the war years*

Годо́в is only used with ordinals, as in:

лю́ди сороковы́х годо́в	*the Men of the 'Forties*

Го́ды (*nom.* and *acc.pl.*) and **года́м, года́ми, о года́х** are used normally, with both ordinals and other adjectives:

в вое́нные го́ды	*during the war years*
в ва́ши го́ды	*at your age*

Note also:

на ста́рости лет	*in one's old age*
челове́к сре́дних лет	*a middle-aged person*

54

(ii) USE OF **человéк**

The genitive plural **человéк** is used with cardinal numbers:

пять человéк, сто человéк, тысяча человéк

and **людéй** with words of quantity:

мнóго людéй, большинствó людéй

however, with **скóлько** and **нéсколько, человéк** is used:

скóлько человéк, нéсколько человéк

§70 DIFFERENCES

The difference between two figures is expressed by **на** + *acc*.[1]:

Он стáрше брáта на пять лет.

He is five years older than his brother.

Этот дом на одúн этáж вы́ше нáшего.

This house is one storey higher than ours.

Phrases such as 'so many times bigger' are expressed by **в** + *acc.*:

Он в два рáза (вдвóе) стáрше брáта.

He is twice as old as his brother.

Территóрия СССР приблизúтельно в три рáза бóльше территóрии США.

The U.S.S.R. is approximately three times the size of (bigger than) the U.S.A.

§71 DIMENSIONS

Длинá, *length;* **ширинá,** *breadth;* **высотá,** *height;* **глубинá,** *depth,* are used as follows:

Какóй длины́ (ширины́, глубины́) эта рекá?

How long (wide, deep) is this river?

Эта рекá длинóй в девятьсóт киломéтров. (Длинá этой реки́ — девятьсóт киломéтров.)

This river is nine hundred kilometres long.

Эта рекá местáми **в** одúн киломéтр ширинóй (одúн киломéтр в ширину́).

In places this river is one kilometre wide.

Глубинá этой реки́ дохóдит до пятúдесяти мéтров.

This river is up to fifty metres deep.

---

[1] The instrumental is also used:

одни́м гóдом (двумя́ годáми, etc.) стáрше, и т.д.

Какóй высоты́ эта горá?

How high is this mountain?

Эта горá высотóй в три ты́сячи мéтров. (Эта горá в три ты́сячи мéтров высоты́. Высотá этой горы́ — три ты́сячи мéтров.)

This mountain is three thousand metres high.

Самолёт подня́лся на высоту́ двух ты́сяч мéтров.

The aeroplane rose to a height of two thousand metres.

Он летéл на высотé двух ты́сяч мéтров.

It was flying at a height of two thousand metres.

§72 DISTANCE

(i) **От . . . до** express the distance between two places:

От Лóндона до Ду́вра пятьдеся́т миль.

It is fifty miles from London to Dover.

(ii) **Из . . . в, с . . . на** express the journey made from one place to another:

Мы éхали из Лóндона в Дувр (с Кавкáза на Украи́ну).

We were travelling from London to Dover (from the Caucasus to the Ukraine).

(iii) **От . . . к** are commonly used of the road leading from one place to another. **Из . . . в** are also used:

Эта дорóга ведёт от Лóндона к Ду́вру.

This road leads from London to Dover.

Дорóга из Москвы́ в Загóрск (дорóга на Загóрск).

The road from Moscow to Zagorsk.

For Expressions of Time with *from . . . to*, see §162.

§73 **B** +*prep.* followed by **от** +*gen.* expresses the distance away from a place or person:

Он стоя́л в четырёх мéтрах (шагáх, я́рдах) от меня́.

He was standing four yards from me.

Лóдка остановилась в трёх киломéтрах от бéрега.

The boat stopped three kilometres from the shore.

Óзеро находи́лось киломéтрах в десяти́ к ю́гу от гóрода.

The lake was some ten kilometres south of the city.

Pronouns

§74 USE OF ЭТО

(i) Это (*this is, it is, these are*, etc.,) standing first in the sentence, is used as preliminary subject preceding the verb. The actual subject follows the verb.

Это is not declined, being unaffected by the gender or number of the actual subject. The verb is governed by the latter:

Это мой брат (моя сестра).	*This is my brother* (*sister*).
Это **была** очень интересная пьеса.	*It was a very interesting play.*
Это **были** мои друзья.	*These were my friends.*
Это **будут** приятные новости для него.	*This will be pleasant news for him.*

In a negative statement with **это не** the actual subject is NOT in the genitive:

Это не его брат.	*This* (*it*) *is not his brother.*
Это не был его брат.	*This* (*it*) *was not his brother.*
Это не была интересная пьеса.	*It was not an interesting play.*

Since the noun following **быть** is the subject it cannot stand in the instrumental.

If the predicate is an adjective, it is in the short form:

Это (было) очень интересно.	*It is* (*was*) *very interesting.*

There are, however, some occasions when **это** is both the logical and the grammatical subject, representing the sum total of the preceding sentence:

В 1957-ом году он был назначен министром иностранных дел. **Это было вершиной** его политической карьеры.

In 1957 he was appointed Foreign Secretary. This was the climax of his political career.

(ii) **Э́то** is not used in such expressions as:

Не секре́т, что . . .	*It is no secret that . . .*
Сего́дня хо́лодно.	*It is cold today.*
День был хоро́ший.	*It was a nice day.*
Стоя́ла прекра́сная весе́нняя пого́да.	*It was beautiful spring weather.*
Была́ зима́, э́то бы́ло зимо́й (or simply зима́).	*It was winter.*

In translating pleonastic expressions like:

It was only then that I became interested in Russia,

all unnecessary words are omitted:

То́лько **тогда́** я по-настоя́щему заинтересова́лся Росси́ей.

Э́то **я** взял де́ньги.	*It was I who took the money.*
Кто э́то прохо́дит ми́мо до́ма?	*Who is that passing the house?*
Э́то о **вас** говоря́т.	*It is you they are talking about.*
Не **э́то** трево́жило её.	*This was not what troubled her.*

Such statements may also be rendered by inverted word order (cf. §17):

Гла́вной причи́ной войны́ была́ агресси́вная поли́тика Герма́нии.

It was German aggressive policy that was the chief cause of the war.

For the emphatic use of **э́то**, see §§12, 123.

§75 Кото́рый, кто, что (relative)

(i) **Кото́рый** is used when the antecedent is a noun:

Мужчи́на, кото́рый сиде́л ря́дом со мной, чита́л газе́ту.
The man who was sitting next to me was reading a paper.

The GENDER and NUMBER of **кото́рый** are those of its antecedent in the main clause; its CASE is determined within the relative clause:

Вы зна́ете мужчи́ну, кото́рый сиде́л ря́дом со мной?
Do you know the man who was sitting next to me?

Мужчи́на, кото́рого я встре́тил на конце́рте, был ру́сский.
The man whom I met at the concert was a Russian.

Вот мужчи́на, о кото́ром я говори́л.
This is the man I was talking about.

Note that **кото́рый** is used less commonly as an interrogative adjective or pronoun; which . . . ? and what . . . ? being normally rendered by **како́й** . . .

Кака́я ва́ша люби́мая кни́га? *Which is your favourite book?*

В како́м го́роде вы живёте? *In which town do you live?*

but:

Кото́рый час? *What is the time?*

В кото́ром часу́ . . . ? *At what time . . . ?*

(ii) When the antecedent is a pronoun, **кто** and **что** are used:

Все, кто смотре́л пье́су, оста́лись о́чень дово́льны (ей).
All those who saw the play were very pleased with it.

but:

Лю́ди, кото́рые смотре́ли пье́су . . .
The people who saw the play . . .

Note that **кто** is followed by a masculine singular verb irrespective of the subject of the main clause.

Челове́к, о кото́ром (or тот, о ком) вы говори́те, мой друг.
The person you are talking about is a friend of mine.

То, что вы говори́те, о́чень интере́сно.
What you are saying is very interesting.

Я вам рассказа́л всё, что зна́ю.
I have told you all I know.

Что is also used when referring to the whole of the preceding statement:

Он неме́дленно предложи́л помо́чь мне, что меня́ о́чень обра́довало.
He offered to help me at once; which made me very happy.

Сам, са́мый AND себя́; друг дру́га

§76 Сам (сама́, само́, са́ми) is an emphatic pronoun; it stands in apposition to, and agrees with, another pronoun or noun in number, gender and case. It translates *myself, itself, on my own*, etc. It must be clearly distinguished from the reflexive **себя́**; see §78(i).

Сам учи́тель не знал.
Even the teacher (the teacher himself) did not know.

Я сам э́то сде́лаю.

I will do it myself (on my own).

Вы же са́ми зна́ете, что э́то не так.

You know yourself that this is wrong.

Я по́дал письмо́ самому́ заве́дующему.

I handed the letter to the manager himself.

Вы реши́ли э́ту зада́чу са́ми? — (Да,) сам.

Did you solve this problem on your own? Yes, I did.

Суди́те са́ми.

Judge for yourself.

(Мне) хо́чется идти́ самому́.

I feel like going myself.

Я его́ не звала́ к себе́, он сам пришёл. [Че́хов]

I didn't invite him here, he came of his own accord.

NOTE. **Сам** is sometimes used in the second of two main clauses, both of which have the same person for their subject; **сам** indicates that the action in the second clause is of greater personal relevance to the subject than that in the first:

Же́нщина приказа́ла ребёнку сесть к столу́, а сама́ всё стои́т у две́ри, как бу́дто она́ чужа́я.

The woman told the child to sit down at the table, and went on standing by the door, as though she were a stranger there.

§77 Very similar in form is **са́мый (-ая, -ое, -ые)**. Note the fixed stress. It is used:

(i) In expressions giving precise location (*in the very centre of, right on the edge of, just by*, etc.):

Они́ жи́ли в са́мом це́нтре го́рода.

They lived right in the centre of the town.

Маши́на останови́лась у са́мого крыльца́.

The car stopped right by the front porch.

Жил стари́к с свое́ю стару́хой

У са́мого си́него мо́ря.   [Пу́шкин]

An old man and his wife lived right by the edge of the blue sea.

(ii) In superlatives: **са́мый интере́сный, са́мый прия́тный**; see §54.

(iii) It only means *same* in conjunction with **тот же**. It is, moreover, often left out:

60

Это был тот же самый человек, которого мы встретили в поезде.
It was the same man that we had met on the train.

Мы учились в той же школе.   *We went to the same school.*

Всего хорошего! — Вам того же![1]
All the best! The same to you!

In a negative statement **не тот** is used:

Теперь, брат, я не тот. [Грибоедов]
I am a different person (lit. *not the same*) *now, my friend.*

Same is also expressed by **один**, see §56.

§78 (i) The reflexive **себя** (*self*) has no gender or number nor has it a nominative case. Thus it can never be the subject of a sentence. Like **свой** (see §47) it refers to the subject of the sentence or CLAUSE:

Я спрашивал себя.   *I wondered* (lit. *asked myself*).

Он спрашивал себя.   *He wondered.*

Я (он) думал только о себе.
I (*he*) *was only thinking about myself* (*himself*).

Я (он) купил себе новое пальто.
I (*he*) *bought myself* (*himself*) *a new coat.*

Он любит говорить о самом себе.
He loves talking about himself.

Мы взяли брата с собой.
We took my brother with us.

Мы говорили между собой.
We were talking among ourselves.

but:

Это между нами.
This is between you and me (i.e. *confidentially*).

С характерной для **него** вежливостью Давид встал и предложил незнакомцу место. (See §47, Note 1.)
With typical courtesy, David got up and offered the stranger his seat.

Мальчик попросил мать налить **ему** молока. (See §47, Note 2.)
The boy asked his mother to pour him some milk.

See also §48.

[1] Genitive after **желаю**, which is understood.

(ii) **Друг дру́га** (*each other*)

The first word is indeclinable: **друг дру́гу**, *to each other*; **друг от дру́га**, *from each other*; **друг с дру́гом**, *with each other*, etc.

SOME, ANY, ETC.

§79 The suffixes **–то** and **–нибудь** can be added to any interrogative pronoun, adjective or adverb:

кто — кто́-то, кто́-нибудь; что — что́-то, что́-нибудь; какой — какой-то, какой-нибудь; где—где́-то, где́-нибудь, etc.

The resultant words are indefinite pronouns, adjectives and adverbs. Of the two suffixes, **–то** is the more specific, **–нибудь** the more general.[1]

Кто́-то, *someone*, denotes one and one person only. It is indefinite in that he is unknown or remains anonymous:

Сего́дня у́тром кто́-то заходи́л за ва́ми, но он не назва́л своего́ и́мени.
Somebody called for you this morning, but he did not leave his name.

Я дал письмо́ кому́-то в конто́ре.
I gave the letter to somebody in the office.

Где́-то, когда́-то, давны́м-давно́ тому́ наза́д, я прочита́л одно́ стихотворе́ние . . . [Турге́нев]
Somewhere, sometime, many years ago, I read a certain poem . . .

§80 Кто́-нибудь may be anyone out of an unspecified number of persons and does not suggest that a particular person is borne in mind. It is especially common with the imperative and the future tense:

Закро́йте дверь скоре́е! Кто́-нибудь мо́жет уви́деть нас.
Shut the door quickly! Somebody may see us.

Да́йте письмо́ кому́-нибудь в конто́ре.
Give the letter to someone in the office.

Завтра почита́ем что-нибудь из Чехова.
Tomorrow we'll read something by Chekhov.

Compare:

Я расскажу́ вам что́-то о Росси́и.
I will tell you something about Russia.

[1] The suffix **-либо** is virtually identical in meaning with **-нибудь** but is less frequently used.

Расскажи́те нам что́-нибудь о Росси́и.

Tell us something about Russia.

Где живёт Воло́дя? — Он живёт где́-то за́ городом.

Where does Volodya live? He lives somewhere in the country.

Мне хоте́лось бы жить где́-нибудь за́ городом.

I should like to live somewhere in the country.

Почему́-то его́ нет до́ма.

For some reason he is not in.

Да́йте мне знать, е́сли почему́-нибудь не смо́жете прийти́.

Let me know if for any reason you can't come.

The prefix **кое–** is also used to form indefinite adverbs, etc.: **кое-где́,** *here and there*; **кое-ка́к,** '*any old how*'; **кое-где́ видне́лись цветы́; рабо́та сде́лана кое-ка́к.**

§81 SOME

(i) If *some* expresses a limited quantity of physical objects the partitive genitive is used (see §22):

Да́йте хле́ба.

Give me some bread.

Contrast: **да́йте хлеб** (*the bread*) and **да́йте хле́ба** (*some bread*).

(ii) **Како́й-то, како́й-нибудь**

Compare:

Вчера́ я ви́дел како́й-то америка́нский фильм.

Yesterday I saw some American film (or other).

Пойдём посмо́трим како́й-нибудь америка́нский фильм.

Let's go and see some American film (any one at all).

Како́й-то often translates the indefinite article (cf. **оди́н,** §56):

Кто вам сказа́л? — Мне сказа́л како́й-то мужчи́на.

Who told you? A man told me.

Вас спра́шивал како́й-то мужчи́на; он оста́вил для вас каку́ю-то кни́гу.

A man asked to see you; he left a book for you.

See also §14.

(iii) **Не́сколько** (+*gen.*): **не́сколько неде́ль тому́ наза́д,** *some (a few) weeks ago*; **не́сколько домо́в,** *some (a few) houses.*

(iv) *Some* may be omitted in translation when quantity is not stressed, or when it performs the functions of an indefinite plural article (cf. French *des*):

У меня́ бы́ли де́ньги.

I had some money.

Она́ вы́шла купи́ть мя́со.

She went out to buy some meat.

Вдали́ я уви́дел корабли́ (не́сколько кораблей).

I saw some ships in the distance.

(v) **Не́который**, *some, a certain*:

Я находи́лся в не́котором затрудне́нии.

I was in some difficulties.

Не́которые ду́мают не так.

Some people think otherwise.

For *some* with approximate number, see §62.

§82 ANY

This word may have a meaning closer to *all kinds of, every*:

Э́ту кни́гу вы мо́жете доста́ть в любо́м (во вся́ком) кни́жном магази́не.

You can get this book in any bookshop.

Возьми́те любу́ю кни́гу.	*Take any book.*
Э́то поймёт вся́кий.	*Anybody will understand.*
без вся́ких затрудне́ний	*without any difficulty*
в любо́е вре́мя	*at any time*
во вся́ком слу́чае	*in any case*
лу́чше всех (see §54)	*better than anyone else*

Any is omitted when quantity is not emphasised:

У вас есть де́ньги?	*Have you any money?*
Есть вопро́сы?	*Are there any questions?*

For the use of *any*, etc. with negatives, see §§148-50.

The Verb

SOME USES OF TENSES

For the use of the future after **éсли, когда́**, see §117; with **быва́ло**, §125.

§83 THE ENGLISH PERFECT CONTINUOUS ('have been going', etc.)

This is usually rendered by the present tense, since the action described is still going on. **Уже́** or **всего́** are often added:

Мы живём здесь уже́ три го́да.
We have been (and still are) living here for three years.

Мы изуча́ем ру́сский язы́к всего́ два го́да.
We have been learning Russian for only two years.

Я жду (ждал) его́ це́лый час.
I have (had) been waiting for him for a whole hour.

§84 The present tense is also used with **давно́**, *for a long time*:

Мы уже́ давно́ знако́мы.	*We have known each other for a long time.*
Он давно́ здесь?	*Has he been here long?*
Я их зна́ю давно́.	*I have known them for a long time.*

but:

Я их знал давно́.	*I* HAD *known them for a long time.*

Давно́ (давны́м-давно́) with the past tense also means *long ago*:

Э́ту кни́гу я купи́л давно́.	*I bought this book long ago.*
Я давно́ забы́л об э́том.	*I have forgotten about this ages ago.*

The past tense is also used with NEGATIVE verbs of the type:

Я уже́ давно́ не получа́ла письма́ от него́.	*I have not heard from him for a long time.* (See §99.)

Неда́вно means both *not long* and *recently*; **давно́ не**, *not for a long time*. Compare:

Он здесь неда́вно.	*He has not been here long.*

65

Он давно́ здесь не́ был.	*He has not been here for a long time.*
Он был здесь неда́вно.	*He was here recently.*

§85 До́лго as distinct from **давно́** does not imply the continuity of an action or condition from the past into the present:

Вчера́ он до́лго рабо́тал.	*Yesterday he worked for a long time.*
Он до́лго обе́дал, он до́лго сиде́л за обе́дом.[1]	*He took a long time over his dinner.*

§86 THE ENGLISH PLUPERFECT

Owing to the absence of this tense in Russian, explanatory adverbs or adverbial phrases are inserted into the sentence. Note the following:

All the guests had gone when Semyonov appeared.

Все го́сти ушли́, когда́ Семёнов появи́лся could mean that the guests left the moment Semyonov appeared. In order to clarify that their departure preceded his arrival, **уже́** is inserted:

Все го́сти **уже́** ушли́, когда́ Семёнов появи́лся.

Similarly:

Мы **уже́** е́хали не́сколько часо́в, когда́ я вспо́мнил, что я забы́л письмо́.

We had been travelling for several hours when I remembered that I had forgotten the letter.

Стари́к, с кото́рым я говори́л, **в мо́лодости** был чле́ном Комсомо́ла.

The old man I spoke to had been a member of the Komsomol.

Without **ра́ньше, в мо́лодости, в своё вре́мя**, etc. the statement would be nonsensical. Another example:

In 1956 they moved into a large house that had been built recently.

В 1956-о́м году́ они́ перее́хали в большо́й дом, кото́рый был постро́ен неда́вно might mean *which was built recently*, i.e. shortly before this passage was written. For clarity's sake, use **незадо́лго до э́того** or **то́лько что**:

. . . они́ перее́хали в большо́й дом, кото́рый был то́лько что постро́ен (кото́рый был постро́ен незадо́лго до э́того).

---

[1] **Он до́лго обе́дает** is either a 'vivid' present (action in progress), or describes a characteristic feature: *he (always) takes a long time over his dinner.*

§87 THE TENSE IN INDIRECT STATEMENTS

The tense in an indirect statement or question is what it was in the original (direct) statement or question. Compare:

Он сказа́л: «Я приду́ че́рез неде́лю.»
He said: 'I'll come in a week's time.'

Он сказа́л, что (он) придёт че́рез неде́лю.
He said that he would come in a week's time.

Я спроси́л его́: «Где вы живёте?»
I asked him: 'Where do you live?'

Я спроси́л его́, где он живёт.
I asked him where he lived.

Он сказа́л, что (он) зна́ет моего́ бра́та.
He said that he knew my brother.

Я спра́шивал себя́, где я ви́дел его́ пре́жде.
I wondered where I had seen him before.

Я спра́шивал себя́, отчего́ он избега́ет нас.
I wondered why he had been avoiding us.

Она́ сказа́ла, что (она́) уже́ пять лет за́мужем.
She said she had been married for five years.

Он писа́л, что (он) живёт в Пари́же, но ча́сто приезжа́ет в А́нглию; так как он бу́дет в Ло́ндоне в нача́ле ма́я, он наде́ется, что уда́стся встре́титься где́-нибудь.
He wrote to say that he was living in Paris, but often came to England; as he would be in London at the beginning of May, he hoped that we would be able to meet somewhere.

(For Indirect Command, see §115(ii); for Conditionals, §§116-19.)

The use of tenses is similar after the verbs *to think, to feel*, etc.:

Мне показа́лось, что пора́ идти́.
I thought it was time to go.

Я почу́вствовал, что что́-то нела́дно.
I felt that something was wrong.

Я наде́ялся, что вы придёте.   *I hoped you would come.*

§88 *If* and *whether* in an indirect question are translated by the enclitic ли (not е́сли); *whether ... or* by ли ... и́ли (же). Cf. §19.

Я спроси́л его́, лю́бит ли он му́зыку.
I asked him whether he liked music.

Cáша спроси́л нас, хоти́м ли мы пойти́ в теа́тр и́ли же оста́ться до́ма.

Sasha asked us whether we wanted to go to the theatre or stay at home.

Cáша спроси́л нас, понра́вилась ли нам пье́са.

Sasha asked us whether we had enjoyed the play.

Я не знал, пра́вда ли э́то.   *I didn't know whether this was true.*

§89 After the verbs *to see, to hear*, etc. in the past tense, the present tense is the more correct, although the past is also found:

Я слы́шал, как она́ поёт (пе́ла).   *I heard her singing.*

Я ви́дел, как он рабо́тает (рабо́тал) в саду́.

I saw him working in the garden.

Он показа́л мне дом, в кото́ром он живёт.[1]

He showed me the house where he lived.

§90 This use of tenses also applies when a sentence contains a mental monologue rather than a verbal statement:

День его́ рожде́ния (бу́дет) че́рез неде́лю. Придётся посла́ть ему́ откры́тку, и, пожа́луй, купи́ть како́й-нибудь пода́рок.

His birthday was in a week's time. She would have to send him a card and probably buy him a present.

Similarly, in a narrative written in the past tense where a subsequent action is anticipated (*was to*, etc.), the future may be used:

Че́рез не́сколько неде́ль в тако́е же положе́ние попаду́ и я.

A few weeks later I, too, was to find myself in a similar situation.

ASPECTS

I. NORMAL USE OF ASPECTS

§91 (i) The fundamental differences between the two aspects are that the IMPERFECTIVE describes (*a*) an action in progress with no emphasis on its inception or termination, and (*b*) a state of affairs or actions that are habitual or repeated. (But see also §§92, 96.)

The PERFECTIVE describes a single action as qualified in some way, with emphasis on its completion, or, in some cases, on its inception.

The imperfective is used in all three tenses, the perfective normally in the past and future only.

---

[1] в кото́ром он жил could, however, only mean 'where he used to live'.

Normally the perfective differs in form from the imperfective:

(1) By the addition of a prefix: **смотре́ть/посмотре́ть, плати́ть/ заплати́ть**

(2) By change of conjugation from first to second: **получа́ть/ получи́ть, разделя́ть/раздели́ть**

(3) By a change in the stem: **понима́ть/поня́ть (пойму́, пой- мёшь), встава́ть (встаю́, встаёшь)/встать (вста́ну, вста́- нешь)**

(4) By modification of the suffix: **перели́стывать/перелиста́ть, прогу́ливаться/прогуля́ться.**

There are several verbs and verbal groups made up of dissimilar pairs: **уходи́ть/уйти́**, etc., **говори́ть/сказа́ть, брать/взять, лови́ть/пойма́ть, класть/положи́ть, станови́ться/стать, сади́ться/сесть, ложи́ться/лечь,** etc.

Note the similarity in the form of the present tense of many im- perfective verbs and the future of the perfective verb: **я пишу́,** *I write, am writing* and **я напишу́,** *I shall write*; **я получа́ю,** *I receive, am receiving,* and **я получу́,** *I shall receive*; **я иду́,** *I am walking,* **я пойду́,** *I shall go* (from **ходи́ть–идти́/пойти́**) and **я приду́,** *I shall come* (from **приходи́ть/прийти́**).[1]

Compare the use of aspects in the following:

Я обы́чно встаю́ (repeated action, *impfv.*) в семь часо́в, а вчера́ я встал (single action, *pfv.*) в шесть.

Я бу́ду писа́ть (repeated action, *impfv.*) вам ка́ждый день.

Я вам напишу́ (single action, *pfv.*) за́втра.

Я чита́л (action in progress, *impfv.*) кни́гу, когда́ Джон вошёл (single action, *pfv.*) в ко́мнату.

Я прочита́л (completed action, *pfv.*) кни́гу и верну́л (single action, *pfv.*) её в библиоте́ку.

(ii) The IMPERFECTIVE is normally used with adverbs like **до́лго** and **всё ещё,** emphasising action in progress:

Он до́лго говори́л.   *He talked for a long time.*

Он всё ещё спал.   *He was still asleep.*

and with **ча́сто, всегда́, всё, не раз, два ра́за в день,** etc., emphasis- ing repetition:

[1] See §§127, 135.

Он всегда (всё) говорил о вас. *He always spoke about you.*

Это не раз повторялось. *This was repeated more than once.*

Врач заходил два раза в день. *The doctor called twice a day.*

The PERFECTIVE is used with adverbs like **сразу, вдруг, внезапно, немедленно, неожиданно, только что, чуть не**, emphasising immediacy and unity of action[1]:

Вдруг открылась дверь. *Suddenly the door opened.*

Откройте немедленно окно! *Open the window at once!*

Он чуть не засмеялся. *He almost burst out laughing.*

Он только что пришёл. *He has (had) only just come.*

§92 Referring to a single action in the past, a sentence with an IMPERFECTIVE verb may be a simple statement of fact, merely indicating that the action took place. In the following examples specific circumstances or the result of the action are not expressed:

До войны мы жили в Лондоне.
Before the war we lived in London.

Вчера я работал в библиотеке.
Yesterday I worked in the library.

Вы смотрели этот фильм? — Да, смотрел.
Have you seen (did you see) this film? Yes, I have (I did).

The imperfective is also used to express length of time:

Мы жили в Лондоне три года.
We lived in London for three years.

Он работал три часа.
He worked for three hours.

Мы уже шли больше часа.
We had already walked for over an hour.

See also §95(i).

In the title of N. Ostrovsky's book «Как закалялась сталь» (*How the Steel was Tempered*) the verb is imperfective because what is

---

[1] The imperfective is, of course, used in the present tense and when the action is habitual:

Вдруг он встаёт и подходит к ней.
Suddenly he gets up and goes up to her.

Каждый раз, увидев её, он сразу вставал и подходил к ней.
Every time he saw her, he got up at once and went up to her.

70

described is the gradual progress of the action and not its completion. Similarly:

Он рассказа́л нам, как отдыха́л ле́том.
He told us how he had spent his summer holidays.

Мы е́хали ме́дленно по доро́ге.
We drove slowly along the road.

§93 Whereas the imperfective (in the past tense) merely states that an action took place (see §92 above), the PERFECTIVE makes the statement more specific:

Вы вчера́ звони́ли? — Да, звони́л.
Did you phone yesterday? Yes, I did.

but:

Я позвони́л ему́, что́бы вы́яснить э́тот вопро́с.
I phoned him in order to clear this matter up.

See also §97.

If it is stated precisely how many times an action is performed, the perfective is normally used:

Он постуча́л три ра́за в дверь.
He knocked at the door three times.

The imperfective is used if the number is left vague:

Он стуча́л мно́го раз в дверь.
He knocked at the door many times.

The perfective is also used with repeated actions when each action is clearly a completed one and when they were all completed on the same occasion:

Вчера́ я написа́л три письма́ (шесть, мно́го пи́сем).
Yesterday I wrote three (six, many) letters.

These letters were written on one and the same occasion and each was completed and ready to be posted. **Вчера́ я писа́л друзья́м пи́сьма** means that I did spend some time writing letters but it does not make it clear whether I completed them.

§94 (i) Two simultaneous actions are expressed by the imperfective:

Я сиде́л у окна́ и слу́шал му́зыку.
I sat by the window and listened to the music.

When enumerating several consecutive actions the perfective is used:

Мы пообéдали в ресторáне, вы́пили по три и́ли четы́ре стакáна пи́ва, погуля́ли по гóроду, и верну́лись домóй пóздно вéчером.

We had dinner at a restaurant, had three or four glasses of beer, walked round the town and returned home late at night.

The change from one state to another is also expressed by the perfective:

Сначáла ру́сская пи́ща нам не нрá вилась, но потóм (онá) понрá вилась.

At first we did not like Russian food, but after a while we came to like it.

Пóезд сначáла шёл óчень мéдленно, но затéм (он) пошёл быстрée (=набрáл скóрость).

At first the train moved very slowly, but then it gathered speed.

(ii) The two aspects also differ in that the imperfective may suggest the idea of *I strove, was trying to,* and the perfective *I did, succeeded in doing.*

Мы дóлго уговá ривали егó, но не уговори́ли.

We tried to persuade him for a long time, but did not succeed.

Весь день он лови́л ры́бу, но он ничегó не поймáл.

He spent all day fishing, but did not catch anything.

Он добивáется (добивá лся) признáния.

He is trying (was trying) to gain recognition.

Он доби́лся признáния.

He gained recognition.

Similarly:

Он добивáлся тогó, чтóбы ему́ дá ли нóвую кварти́ру.

Он доби́лся тогó, что ему́ дáли нóвую кварти́ру.

§95 SPECIFIC FUNCTIONS OF SOME PERFECTIVE FORMS

(i) Semantically there is normally no difference between the two aspects of a verb. However, the prefix **по-**, in addition to providing the perfective aspect of many simple verbs, can add the restrictive meaning *for a little while*:

Мы посидéли (нéкоторое врéмя).	*We sat for a while.*
Мы побесéдуем.	*We will have a chat.*

With verbs of motion **по-** adds the meaning *set out*, etc.:

Он пошёл домой (не зна́ю, дошёл ли он).	*He went home (I don't know whether he GOT home).*
Пошли́! (Пое́хали!)	*We are off!*
Вдруг пошёл дождь.	*Suddenly it started to rain.*

Compare §134.

In certain verbs the prefix **за-**, in addition to providing the perfective aspect, also adds the meaning *begin*:

Она́ запла́кала.	*She burst into tears.*
(Моё) се́рдце заби́лось быстре́е.	*My heart began to beat faster.*
Он закури́л папиро́су.	*He lit a cigarette.*
Вдруг пти́цы запе́ли.	*Suddenly the birds began to sing.*

With many verbs (e.g. **жить, стоя́ть, сиде́ть**) the perfective with **про-** may be used. It conveys the meaning of completed action, making the expression of time virtually a direct object (cf. §92):

Я про́жил (=провёл) три го́да в Ло́ндоне.
I lived (spent) three years in London.

Так они́ простоя́ли мину́т пять.
Thus they stood for about five minutes.

Perfective verbs with the suffix **-нуть** indicate a brief, single action carried out instantaneously:

Он кри́кнул: «Осторо́жно!» *He called out: 'Be careful!'*

Other forms of the perfective also exist: **закрича́ть**, *to start shouting*; **покрича́ть**, *to shout for some time*.

Similarly:

стуча́ть/постуча́ть, застуча́ть, сту́кнуть	*to knock*
сверка́ть/посверка́ть, засверка́ть, сверкну́ть	*to flash*
пры́гать/попры́гать, запры́гать, пры́гнуть	*to jump*

(ii) The past tense of the perfectives **уви́деть, услы́шать** is only used when there is an element of suddenness or surprise:

Вы ви́дели э́тот фильм? — Да, мы ви́дели его́ вчера́.
Have you seen this film? Yes, we saw it yesterday.

Заверну́в за́ угол, мы уви́дели пе́ред собо́й большо́й бе́лый дом.
Turning the corner we saw a large white house before us.

73

Мы слы́шали, как она́ поёт.	*We heard (could hear) her sing.*
Идя́ по доро́ге, мы услы́шали плач ребёнка.	*Walking along the road we heard the cry of a child.*

This does NOT apply to the future:

Я уви́жу вас за́втра.	*I shall see you tomorrow.*
Постучи́те погро́мче, а то не услы́шат (не слы́шно).	*Knock louder or they won't hear you.*

Знать is *to know*, **узна́ть** is *to get to know, find out*:

Вы зна́ете, когда́ по́езд придёт? — Нет, но узна́ю.

Узнава́ть/узна́ть is *to recognise*:

Когда́ она́ хо́дит в э́той шля́пе, её не узнаю́т (*pres. impfv.*).

В э́той шля́пе её не узна́ют (*fut. pfv.*).

The colloquial imperfectives **вида́ть** and **слыха́ть** are used in the past tense and infinitive only: **Вы э́то зна́ли? — Ка́жется, слыха́л** (*I may have heard about it some time*). They are used in particular with the negative and have the force of *never at all*: **Вы ви́дели э́ту о́перу? — Нет, не вида́л.**

§96 The use of aspects is brought out in the following examples:

Что вы де́лали сего́дня? — Я ходи́ла в го́род за поку́пками.
What did you do today? I went to town and did some shopping.

If the question had been **Что вы сде́лали сего́дня?** the answer would have been **Ничего́** unless something definite had been achieved, e.g.

Я дописа́л своё сочине́ние.　　*I finished my essay.*

Also:

Что же де́лал Бе́льтов в продолже́ние э́тих десяти́ лет? Всё и́ли почти́ всё. Что он сде́лал? Ничего́ и́ли почти́ ничего́. [Ге́рцен]

What did Beltov do during these ten years? Everything, or almost everything. What did he achieve? Nothing, or almost nothing.

Similarly:

(*a*) Вы чита́ли газе́ту?	*Have you read the paper?*
(*b*) Вы прочита́ли газе́ту?	

In the case of (*a*) the questioner wants to know whether you are familiar with the contents of the paper, while in (*b*) he merely wishes to know whether you have finished with it. Therefore the conversation could continue:

(*a*) Да, чита́л. — Тогда́ скажи́те, что́ сего́дня но́вого.

or: (*b*) Да, прочита́л. — Тогда́ да́йте её мне, пожа́луйста.

Similarly:

Вы обе́дали? — Да, обе́дал. *Have you had dinner? Yes, I have.*

Вы пообе́дали? — Да, пообе́дал.
Have you finished your dinner? Yes, I have.

Potential and anticipated actions are expressed by the imperfective:

Он бежа́л на ста́нцию, так как опа́здывал на по́езд.
He ran to the station, as he was late for the train.

Так как он опозда́л на по́езд, он верну́лся домо́й.
As he had missed the train, he went back home again.

Он сиде́л до́ма, так как на друго́й день сдава́л экза́мен.
He stayed at home, as he had an examination on the following day.

II. IDIOMATIC USES OF ASPECTS[1]

§97 As will have been seen, the use of aspects is largely a matter of emphasis. The following examples illustrate how various elements of a sentence are stressed by the use of aspects:

Мой друг **написа́л** мне интере́сное письмо́.
My friend wrote me an interesting letter.

(Here the main emphasis is not on the act of writing, but on the letter, the direct object; hence PERFECTIVE.)

Мой друг **писа́л**, что прие́дет ко мне (в го́сти).
My friend wrote to say that he was coming to visit me.

(The IMPERFECTIVE here makes the act of writing as important as the content of the letter and makes it more immediate and relevant to the speaker personally.)

В 1919-ом году́ Серге́й Петро́вич **написа́л** дру́гу, что перее́хал в Москву́.

In 1919 Sergei Petrovich wrote to a friend that he had moved to Moscow.

(An objective, impersonal statement of fact set in the distant past; hence PERFECTIVE.)

Вы **купи́ли** биле́ты?   *Did you buy any tickets?*

(Here the emphasis is on the result of the action, i.e. on the direct object; hence PERFECTIVE.)

[1] The remarks in this and the following paragraphs (97-9) apply to the past tense only.
It must also be remembered that various types of verbs are influenced by aspects in different ways, and it would be a mistake to apply these remarks indiscriminately to all verbs.

Кто **покупáл** билéты?   *Who bought the tickets?*

(It is obviously known that the action has been performed; the questioner wishes to know who did the buying; hence IMPERFECTIVE.)

Он **кончáл** университéт, не бросáя рабóту в шкóле.

He took his degree without giving up his teaching post.

(Emphasis on the circumstances under which the action was performed; hence IMPERFECTIVE.)

Он **кóнчил** университéт в 1956-óм годý.

He took his degree in 1956.

(Emphasis is on the completion of the action; hence PERFECTIVE).

NOTE. In certain verbs of saying (**говори́ть/сказáть, отвечáть/отвéтить**) when introducing a direct statement, the difference between the two aspects is not always maintained. There is very little difference between «**Порá вставáть**», — сказáл мой товáрищ and «**Порá вставáть**», — говори́л мой товáрищ.

§98 When an action in the past is wholly divorced from the present or the time of speaking, the imperfective is used. When the action is of relevance to the present or time of speaking, the perfective is used:

Я брал э́ту кни́гу из библиотéки.

I borrowed this book from the library (but returned it).

Я взял э́ту кни́гу из библиотéки.

I borrowed this book from the library (and it is still in my possession).

Брат приезжáл ко мне.

My brother came to see me (but has gone again).

Брат приéхал ко мне.

My brother has come to see me (and is staying with me).

Вчерá я заходи́л к вам, но вас нé было дóма; вот я и зашёл опя́ть.

I called on you yesterday, but you were out. So I have called again.

Я вам говори́л об э́том.

I told you about this (some time ago).

Я вам (тóлько что) сказáл об э́том.

I told you about this (just now).

Отчегó вы не откры́ли окнá? Здесь óчень дýшно. — Я же открывáла окнó.

Why haven't you opened the window? It's very stuffy here. — But I've had it open.

§99 Aspects are used with NEGATIVE verbs in much the same way as with positive verbs, though there is a tendency to use the imperfective:

Мы ждáли егó цéлый день, но он не приходúл (but: а он пришёл тóлько пóздно вéчером).

We waited for him all day, but he did not come (and he did not come till late at night).

Вы купúли газéту? — Нет, не покупáл.

Did you buy a paper? No, I didn't.

Я не знáю, кто взял вáшу кнúгу; я, по крáйней мéре, не брал.

I don't know who took your book; I didn't, anyway.

See also §§ 100, 101.

§100 The use of aspects applies equally to other forms of the verb, i.e. the participles, gerunds and the infinitive (for the imperative, see §101).

(i) Читáя кнúгу, ...   *While reading the book ...*

Прочитáв кнúгу, ...   *Having read the book ...*

Мáльчик, читáвший кнúгу, ...   *The boy who was reading the book ...*

Мáльчик, прочитáвший кнúгу, ...   *The boy who had finished the book ...*

See §§ 105, 112.

(ii) Usage with the infinitive:

Я хочý встрéтить вас ещё раз.

I want to meet you once more.

Бы́ло бы хорошó встречáть вас кáждую недéлю.

It would be nice to meet you every week.

Я прошý вас помóчь мне.

I am asking you to help me (on this occasion).

Я прошý вас помогáть мне.

I am asking you to help me (from now on).

After the verbs *to begin, to continue, to finish*, etc. the IMPERFECTIVE infinitive is always used:

Мы нáчали (стáли) разговáривать.

We started to talk.

Мы продолжáли (кóнчили, перестáли) писáть.

We continued (finished, stopped) writing.

The imperfective is also normally used after the following verbs: учи́ться/вы́-, *to learn*; привыка́ть/привы́кнуть, *to grow accustomed*; устава́ть/уста́ть, *to grow tired*, etc.

The PERFECTIVE infinitive is normally used after успева́ть/успе́ть, *to have time to*; удава́ться/уда́ться, *to succeed*; спеши́ть/по–, *to hurry*; забыва́ть/забы́ть, *to forget*, etc.

A negative infinitive after a positive main verb is generally imperfective:

Я прошу́ вас не говори́ть об э́том.	*I ask you not to speak about this.*
Де́лать бы́ло не́чего.	*There was nothing to be done.*

but:

Он мо́жет не прийти́.	*He may not come.*
Я не мог не заме́тить.	*I could not help noticing.*

There is a tendency to use the imperfective infinitive after не на́до, не сто́ит, etc.:

На́до помо́чь ему́.	*We must help him.*
Не на́до помога́ть ему́.	*We must not (need not) help him.*
Э́тот фильм сто́ит посмотре́ть.	*This film is well worth seeing.*
Э́тот фильм не сто́ит смотре́ть.	*This film is not worth seeing.*

For the infinitive after нельзя́, see §176(ii).

§101 USE OF ASPECTS WITH THE IMPERATIVE

Купи́те что́-нибудь вку́сное на обе́д.
Buy something nice for dinner.

(Всегда́) покупа́йте проду́кты в э́том магази́не.
(Always) buy provisions in this shop.

Принима́йте э́ти табле́тки два ра́за в день.
Take these tablets twice a day.

Скажи́те не́сколько слов.	*Say a few words.*
Говори́те гро́мче.	*Speak louder.*

The negative imperative *do not . . .* is regularly expressed by the IMPERFECTIVE imperative, regardless of the normal functions of aspect:

Купи́те э́ту кни́гу.	*Buy this book.*
Не покупа́йте э́ту кни́гу.	*Don't buy this book.*

78

| Положи́те де́ньги сюда́. | Put the money here. |
| Не клади́те де́нег сюда́. | Don't put the money here. |

However, the perfective imperative is used in warnings that refer to unintentional actions that may take place in the immediate future:

Смотри́, не упади́!	Mind you don't fall!
Не тронь! Горячо́.	Don't touch it! It's hot.
Не разбе́йте их!	Don't break them!
Не забу́дьте.	Don't forget.

Consider the use of aspects in the following:

Откро́йте дверь, пожа́луйста.	Open the door, please.
Запиши́те а́дрес.	Write the address down.
Приходи́те к нам за́втра.	Come and see us tomorrow.
Кури́те, пожа́луйста.	You may smoke.
Сади́тесь, пожа́луйста.	Sit down, please.
Ся́дьте побли́же ко мне.	Sit a little closer to me.
Сиди́те.	Don't get up.
Чита́йте да́льше.	Carry on reading.

The imperfective conveys more urgency than the perfective:

Да́йте мне кни́гу . . . Ну, дава́йте же!
Give me the book . . . Come on, give it to me!

Возьми́те, е́жели (=е́сли) жела́ете . . . Бери́те, богате́йте! [Че́хов]
Take [the jewels] if you want to . . . Go on, take them, make yourself rich!

Встава́й, пульпу́льтик! слы́шишь ли? го́сти! [Го́голь]
Do get up, sweetie! Do you hear me? We have visitors!

§102 The following passage illustrates the use of aspects. The imperfective verbs (in bold type) are used in descriptive, static narrative, giving the setting of the scene. The perfectives (in capital letters) express sudden changes in the situation and action taken by the main character:

Я **е́хал** с охо́ты ве́чером оди́н. Моя́ ло́шадь бо́дро **бежа́ла** по пы́льной доро́ге; уста́лая соба́ка ни на шаг не **отстава́ла** от за́дних колёс. Гроза́ **надвига́лась**. Впереди́ огро́мная лило́вая ту́ча ме́дленно **поднима́лась** из-за ле́су; мне навстре́чу **несли́сь** дли́нные се́рые облака́. Ду́шный жар внеза́пно **СМЕНИ́ЛСЯ** вла́жным хо́лодом; те́ни бы́стро **густе́ли**. Я **УДА́РИЛ** вожжо́й по ло́шади, **СПУСТИ́ЛСЯ** в овра́г, **ПЕРЕБРА́ЛСЯ** че́рез сухо́й ручей, **ПОДНЯ́ЛСЯ** в го́ру и **ВЪЕ́ХАЛ** в лес. Доро́га **вила́сь** пе́редо мно́ю ме́жду густы́ми куста́ми оре́шника; я **подвига́лся** вперёд с трудо́м. Дро́жки **пры́гали** по твёрдым корня́м столе́тних дубо́в и лип; ло́шадь моя́ **НАЧАЛА́** **спотыка́ться**. Си́льный ве́тер внеза́пно **ЗАГУДЕ́Л** в вышине́, дере́вья **ЗАШУМЕ́ЛИ**, кру́пные ка́пли дождя́ ре́зко **ЗАСТУЧА́ЛИ**, **ЗАШЛЁПАЛИ** по ли́стьям, **СВЕРКНУ́ЛА** мо́лния, и гроза́ **РАЗРАЗИ́ЛАСЬ**. Дождь **ПО́ЛИЛ** ручья́ми. Я **ПОЕ́ХАЛ** ша́гом и ско́ро **ПРИНУЖДЁН БЫЛ ОСТАНОВИ́ТЬСЯ**.

[по И. С. Турге́неву]

In the evening I was driving home after a day's hunting; I was on my own. My horse trotted briskly along the dusty road; my tired dog followed closely behind the rear wheels. A storm was approaching. In front of me a huge purple cloud was slowly rising from behind the forest; long grey clouds came drifting towards me. Suddenly the sultry air became clammy and cold; the shadows deepened quickly. I gave the horse a flick with the reins and descended into a ravine, made my way across a dried-up stream, climbed the other side and entered the forest. The road wound before me between thick hazel bushes; I advanced with difficulty. My carriage bounced on the solid roots of centuries old oak and lime trees; my horse began to stumble. Suddenly a strong wind started to roar overhead, the trees began to rustle and large drops of rain struck the leaves heavily, there was a flash of lightning and the storm broke. The rain poured down in torrents. I slowed down to a walking pace and was soon compelled to stop.

§103 VERBS WITH THE SUFFIX –ся

Verbs with the suffix –ся (–сь) include:

(i) Reflexive verbs, e.g. **мы́ться/вы́–**, *to wash oneself*:

Де́ти вы́мылись и оде́лись.	*The children washed and dressed.*
Мать вы́мыла и оде́ла ребёнка.	*The mother washed and dressed the child.*

(ii) Reciprocal verbs, e.g. **встреча́ться/встре́титься**, *to meet each other*:

Мы встре́тились в го́роде.	*We met in town.*

Я встре́тил её в го́роде or   *I met her in town.*
я встре́тился с ней в го́роде.

(iii) Intransitive verbs, e.g. **начина́ться/нача́ться,** *to begin.* They are used only of events or inanimate beings; the simple form is used if the verb is followed by an infinitive:

Докла́д уже́ начался́.   *The lecture had already begun.*

Докла́дчик уже́ на́чал говори́ть.
The lecturer had already begun to speak.

Докла́д продолжа́лся час.
The lecture went on for an hour.

Докла́д продолжа́л быть интере́сным.
The lecture continued to be interesting.

Дверь откры́лась.   *The door opened.*

Я откры́л дверь.   *I opened the door.*

The suffix **–ся (–сь)** is added to some transitive verbs when they are used absolutely, i.e. without a direct object.

Compare:

Э́та соба́ка куса́ется.   *This dog bites.*

Соба́ка укуси́ла ма́льчику   *The dog bit the boy in the leg.*
    но́гу.

Не толка́йтесь!   *Don't push!*

Кто́-то толка́л меня́ сза́ди.   *Somebody was pushing me from behind.*

Мете́ль хлеста́ла по стена́м и о́кнам, так что всем каза́лось, что снару́жи кто-то толка́ется и цара́пается. [Гайда́р]
The snowstorm was beating against the walls and windows, so that everbody thought someone was pushing and scratching outside.

(iv) Verbs used in a passive sense:

Здесь продаю́тся (продаю́т) хоро́шие проду́кты.
Good provisions are sold here.

Э́то сло́во ча́сто употребля́ется (употребля́ют) непра́вильно.
This word is often used incorrectly.

Пи́сьма в да́льние райо́ны перево́зятся (перево́зят) самолётом.
Mail is flown to distant parts by aircraft.

See also §§109, 110.

(v) Impersonal expressions (see §138):

Мне хо́чется вы́пить.	*I want a drink, I am thirsty.*
Ему́ нездоро́вилось.	*He was not well.*

(vi) Verbs that are not found without the suffix –ся (–сь), many being associated with states of mind, emotions (боя́ться/по–, *to fear*; смея́ться/за–, *to laugh*; улыба́ться/улыбну́ться, *to smile*; любова́ться/по–, *to admire*):

Я не бою́сь его́.	*I am not afraid of him.*
Он смея́лся над ни́ми.	*He laughed at them.*
Мы любова́лись ви́дом.	*We admired the view.*

Note the various uses of verbs ending in –ся in the following sentence:

В до́ме Пу́шкиных собира́лись писа́тели, чита́лись стихи́, говори́лось о литерату́ре.

In the Pushkins' home, writers often gathered, poems were read and literature was discussed.

PARTICIPLES

§104 The functions of a participle, though derived from a verb, are descriptive. It may become an adjective pure and simple:

твой лю́бящий сын	*your loving son*
выдаю́щийся писа́тель	*an outstanding writer*
моя́ люби́мая кни́га	*my favourite book*
откры́тая дверь	*the open door*
мой бы́вший учени́к	*my former pupil*

As such it agrees in number, gender and case with its noun:

Она́ получи́ла письмо́ от одного́ бы́вшего ученика́.
She received a letter from a former pupil.

Ма́льчик чита́л рома́н своего́ люби́мого а́втора.
The boy was reading a novel by his favourite author.

В откры́тую дверь вошли́ два незнако́мца.
Two strangers entered through the open door.

(Of these, only those which were originally PASSIVE participles have a short form; see §108.)

It may become a noun: **учёный**, *scholar*; **заве́дующий, управля́ющий**, *manager*; **сумасше́дший**, *madman*; **трудя́щиеся**, *the toilers.*

§105 Syntactically, a participle or participle clause can replace an entire subordinate clause. As opposed to the gerund (see §112) this clause is invariably a RELATIVE clause. The participle replacing it is in the long form and agrees with its noun, which is outside the participle clause:

Худóжник, написáвший э́ту картúну, у́мер три гóда тому́ назáд.

The artist who painted this picture died three years ago.

Дéвочке, сидя́щей у окнá, дéсять лет.

The girl (who is) sitting by the window is ten years old.

Дéвочке, сидéвшей у окнá, бы́ло дéсять лет.

The girl who was sitting by the window was ten years old.

Мы живём в **большóм дóме, пострóенном** (котóрый был пострóен, котóрый пострóили) два гóда тому́ назáд.

We live in a large house which was built two years ago.

Ю́рий читáл **поэ́му** «Полтáва», **напи́санную** Пу́шкиным (котóрую Пу́шкин написáл) в 1828-óм году́.

Yuri was reading the poem 'Poltava' which Pushkin wrote in 1828.

Одéсса, располóженная на берегу́ Чёрного мóря, явля́ется кру́пным пóртом.

Odessa, situated on the Black Sea, is a major port.

§106 Participle clauses in apposition to pronouns also require the long form of the passive participle (cf. §43):

«Что вы хотúте сказáть?» — спросúл он, озадáченный неожúданным вопрóсом.

'What do you mean?' he asked, puzzled by the unexpected question.

Сопровождáемые (see §107) нáшими друзья́ми, мы пошлú на приём.

Accompanied by our friends we went to the reception.

§107 PRESENT PARTICIPLE PASSIVE

This is not used frequently in spoken Russian, apart from such words as **уважáемый, любúмый** that are now, in effect, adjectives. However, since this is the only IMPERFECTIVE passive participle in common use, it is used in the written language when the action it describes is simultaneous to that of the main verb. (In English this distinction between the present and the past participle passive is not apparent.)

Средú языкóв, изучáемых в нáших шкóлах, францу́зский занимáет вúдное мéсто.

French occupies an important place among the languages studied in our schools.

Contrast:

Армия Наполео́на, пресле́дуемая (*pres. part. pass.*) ру́сскими, едва́ добрала́сь до грани́цы.

Napoleon's army, pursued by the Russians, only just managed to reach the frontier.

with:

Армия Наполео́на, разби́тая (*past part. pass.*) ру́сскими, едва́ добрала́сь до грани́цы.

Napoleon's army, smashed by the Russians, only just managed to reach the frontier.

For punctuation with participle clauses, see §9.

THE PASSIVE VERB

§108 This is formed with the past perfective passive participle in the SHORT form and the appropriate form of **быть** (cf. Short Form of Adjective, §§35 ff.):

Кру́пный порт Оде́сса располо́жен на берегу́ Чёрного мо́ря.

The major port of Odessa is situated on the Black Sea.

Э́тот дом был постро́ен два го́да тому́ наза́д.

This house was built two years ago.

Э́тот дом бу́дет постро́ен че́рез год.

This house will be built in a year's time.

NOTE. There is a difference between **Она́ была́ о́чень смущённа**, *she was very embarrassed* (short form of passive participle used adjectivally, temporary state) and **Она́ была́ смущена́ э́тим неожи́данным вопро́сом,** *she was (had been) embarrassed by this unexpected question* (passive verb, equivalent to **Её смути́л э́тот неожи́данный вопро́с;** see §109, below).

Both **смущённа** and **смущена́** are short forms of **смущённая**, the former virtually an adjective, the latter part of the passive verb. This distinction is not apparent in the masculine (**смущён**).

An adverb, e.g. *excitedly*, is spelt with –**нн**–: **взволно́ванно**; **взволно́вано** is the neuter singular passive of the verb **взволнова́ть**.

In participles formed with the –**т**– stem, the distinction is not apparent. Thus **откры́то** can be the neuter short form of the adjective **откры́тый**, *open*, the neuter singular passive of the verb **откры́ть**, *to open*, or the adverb *openly*. (Cf. §110, below)

§109 Russian commonly uses the active voice where English uses the passive. The word order is that of the English passive sentence (cf. §14):

Траге́дию «Бори́с Годуно́в» написа́л Пу́шкин.

The tragedy Boris Godunov *was written by Pushkin.*

Опыты провёл крупный английский учёный.
The experiments were carried out by a leading British scientist.

Это необходимо сделать сразу.
This must be done at once.

Судья велел (lit. *ordered*) ввести подсудимого.
The judge had the accused brought in.

§110 The reflexive verb is often used in a passive sense with inanimate subjects (see also §103, iv):

Недавно в городе открылся новый театр.
A new theatre was opened in town recently.

Не сразу Москва строилась.
Moscow was not built in a day (lit. *not at once*).

Compare:

Этот музей открыт.	*This museum is open.*
Этот музей открыт недавно.	*This museum has not long been open.*
Этот музей был открыт (открылся, открыли) недавно.	*This museum was opened recently.*

Считаться is used with a passive sense regardless of the nature of the subject:

Иванов считается (Иванова считают) авторитетом в геологии.
Ivan is considered an authority in geology.

«Ревизор» Гоголя вообще считается («Ревизора» . . . считают) одной из лучших комедий мировой литературы.
Gogol's Inspector General *is generally considered one of the finest comedies of world literature.*

Считается фактом, что . . .   *It is considered a fact that . . .*

§111 English passive expressions like *I was told, we were given,* cannot be translated literally, as the dative, which these verbs (**говорить/ сказать, давать/дать,** etc.) govern, must be retained. Translate **мне сказали, мне было сказано; нам дали, нам был дан (была дана,** etc.):

Нам дали по двадцать рублей.
We were given twenty roubles each.

Делайте, как вам сказано.
Do as you are told.

See also §139.

GERUNDS

§112 (i) Gerunds differ from participles in that:

(a) They are indeclinable, being adverbs.

(b) They can only refer to the subject of the sentence or clause.

(c) They are only formed from active verbs, including those ending in –ся (there are no passive gerunds).

(d) There are only two gerunds in common use, the present imperfective and the past perfective; they can be used with main verbs in all three tenses.

(e) They are used both singly and in gerund clauses. In the latter they replace another main clause or a subordinate clause (causal, temporal, descriptive, concessive, conditional, etc., but NOT relative clauses, that is, those introduced by **который, кто** and **что**).

Normal use:

Они́ сиде́ли, разгова́ривая о рабо́те.
They sat talking about their work.

Пообе́дав, мы вы́шли из рестора́на.
When we had finished dinner, we left the restaurant.

Прочита́в кни́гу, я вам дам её.
When I have read the book, I will give it to you.

(ii) The English present gerundive (e.g. 'entering') is often used loosely, when a past gerundive ('having entered') is really meant:

Принеся́[1] поднёс с ча́ем и пече́ньем и поста́вив его́ перед на́ми на стол, официа́нтка спроси́ла нас, жела́ем ли мы ещё чего́-нибудь.
Bringing the tray with tea and biscuits and putting it on the table before us, the waitress asked us whether we wanted anything else.

Compare:

Возвраща́ясь домо́й из го́рода, я встре́тил Алексе́я Петро́вича.
Returning from town I met Alexey Petrovich.

Верну́вшись домо́й из го́рода, я сра́зу лёг спать.
On returning from town I went to bed straight away.

---

[1] While the perfective gerund is normally formed from the past stem (**прочита́л — прочита́в, лёг — лёгши**), with compound verbs of motion this form, derived from the future perfective and using the –я suffix, is the more common. Thus, too, **придя́, увезя́, уведя́** as against the older forms **пришёд(–ши), увёзши, уве́дши.**

Входя́ в ко́мнату, он . . .

Just as he was entering the room he . . .

Войдя́[1] в ко́мнату, он . . .

On entering (having entered) the room he . . .

Perfective gerunds are also used to translate statements like:

He left the room closing the door quietly.

Он вы́шел из ко́мнаты, ти́хо закры́в дверь.

The need for a PERFECTIVE gerund is the first consideration; and the order of the clauses helps to overcome what appears to be a logical inconsistency, when seen from the point of view of tenses. Thus:

Он ушёл, пожа́в плеча́ми. *He went off shrugging his shoulders.*

Пожима́я плеча́ми would mean *continually shrugging his shoulders.*

(iii) The gerund is often used to translate clauses introduced by *before, after, if, unless, by, while,* etc. Note that these conjunctions are NOT translated (but see §167):

Не уби́в медве́дя, шку́ру не дели́.

Don't share out the skin before you've killed the bear.

Не су́йся в во́ду, не зна́я бро́ду.

Look before you leap (lit. don't dive into the water if you don't know where the ford is).

Они́ ушли́, не попроща́вшись с хозя́йкой.

They left without saying goodbye to the hostess.

Рабо́тая день и ночь, он ко́нчил кни́гу во́время.

By working day and night he finished the book in time.

Рабо́тая день и ночь, он (всё-таки) не ко́нчил кни́гу во́время.

Although he worked day and night he did not finish the book in time.

Рабо́тая над э́той кни́гой, он . . .

While working on this book he . . .

Note the use of gerunds in the following:

Я удиви́лся (был удивлён), встре́тив его́ там.

I was surprised to meet him there.

«До за́втра,» — сказа́л он, уходя́.

'See you tomorrow,' he said as he left.

Он лежа́л на крова́ти не разде́вшись.

He was lying on his bed fully clothed.

[1] See footnote, p. 86.

(iv) Expressions like *Sonya stood by the window with her head lowered* are rendered by perfective gerunds:

Со́ня стоя́ла у окна́, опусти́в го́лову.

Gerunds as in:

Музыка́нты, блестя́ ме́дью духовы́х инструме́нтов, уже́ столпи́лись на па́лубе. [И. Бу́нин]

are a Russian equivalent of the English nominative absolute:

The musicians, the brass of their wind-instruments gleaming in the sun, had already crowded on the deck.

§113 In the following sentences gerunds CANNOT be used:

As *we* returned home late at night, *Joan* exclaimed ...
Getting on the train in Moscow, *it* had not occurred to him ...
As *they* waited for the arrival of the Emperor, *a lively conversation* started up among the guests.

Here the subject of the main clause differs from that of the subordinate clause. Hence, either the full subordinate clause must be used (Когда́ мы возвраща́лись домо́й по́здно ве́чером, ... ; когда́ он сади́лся в по́езд в Москве́, ...), or the main clause must be modified (Садя́сь в по́езд в Москве́, он не ду́мал ...).

For punctuation with gerund clauses, see §9.

§114 TRANSLATION OF OTHER WORDS ENDING IN -*ing*

In sentences like *he started (continued, stopped) talking, I like listening to music,* the infinitive is used:

Он на́чал (продолжа́л, переста́л) говори́ть; я люблю́ слу́шать му́зыку.

Note the following constructions:

Я слы́шал, как они́ говори́ли обо мне (see §89).
I could hear them talking about me.

Я не люблю́, когда́ мне меша́ют.
I don't like being disturbed.

Он меша́л мне рабо́тать.
He stopped me working.

Certain expressions involving words ending in -*ing* are best rendered by nouns:

По прие́зде из-за грани́цы ... (see §159).
On arriving from abroad ...

Перед сном...
Before going to bed...

Деревенская жизнь (жизнь в деревне) бывает очень приятной.
Living in the country can be very pleasant.

Этот текст подходит для перевода на русский.
This text is suitable for translating into Russian.

See also §168.

THE SUBJUNCTIVE

§115 The subjunctive is formed with **бы** and **чтобы**, which are used with the PAST TENSE and the INFINITIVE only. Its main uses are:

(i) In wishes and hypothetical statements:

Скорей бы пришло лето! *I wish it were summer soon.*

Я хотел бы поехать в Италию. *I should like to go to Italy.*

Что бы вы делали (сделали) на моём месте?
What would you do (have done) in my place?

(ii) In commands or advice:

Чтобы вы этого больше не делали!
Mind you don't do that again!

Ты бы пошёл спать.
You had better go to bed.

Скажите, господа, чтобы Пётр Иванович не мешал. [Гоголь]
Gentlemen, do tell Pyotr Ivanovich not to interfere.

(iii) With **хотеть/за–; настаивать/настоять; ждать/подо–**, and similar verbs:

Я хочу, чтобы он это знал.[1]
I want him to know this.

Я настаиваю на том, чтобы вы сейчас же пошли домой.
I insist on your going home at once.

Мы ждали, чтобы он вернулся (see §166).
We waited for him to return.

(iv) To express purpose:

Я вам рассказываю это (для того), чтобы вы знали правду.
I am telling you this so that you may know the truth.

[1] **Я хочу его знать** means *I want to know him.*

89

Я éду в Париж (для того), чтобы усовершéнствовать своё знáние францýзского языкá.
I am going to Paris (in order) to improve my French.

Я пригласúл вас, господá, с тем, чтобы сообщúть вам пренеприя́тное извéстие. [Гóголь]
I have invited you, gentlemen, in order to convey to you some most unpleasant news.

After verbs of motion, purpose may be expressed by a plain infinitive:

Я пошёл купúть нóвый гáлстук.
I went to buy a new tie.

Ягнёнок в жáркий день зашёл к ручью́ напúться. [Крылóв]
One hot day a lamb went to the brook to quench its thirst.

(v) With verbs of doubt and fear and often with negative verbs of saying and thinking:

Я сомневáюсь, чтобы э́то бы́ло вéрно.
I doubt whether this is true.

Я бою́сь, чтобы он не пришёл (как бы он не пришёл).
I am afraid that he may come.

but:

Я бою́сь, что он придёт.
I am afraid that he will come.

Я бою́сь, что он мóжет не прийтú (мóжет быть не придёт).
I am afraid that he may not come.

Я не пóмню, чтобы я вúдел егó прéжде.
I cannot remember ever seeing him before.

Я не вéрю, чтобы он мог вестú себя́ так плóхо.
I cannot believe that he can have behaved so badly.

В нём ничегó нет, что напоминáло бы о егó происхождéнии.
There is nothing about him to remind one of his background.

For further uses of **чтобы**, see §§168-70.

(vi) With **бы ... ни**, *whoever, whatever*, etc.:

Кто бы то нú был.
Whoever it may be.

Гдé бы то нú было.
Wherever it may (might) be.

Чтó бы вы ни дéлали, бýдьте осторóжны.
Be careful, whatever you do.

Я прощý емý, чтó бы он ни сдéлал.
I'll forgive him, whatever he has done.

Нельзя́ унывáть, чтó бы ни случи́лось.
You must not lose heart, whatever happens.

Не впускáйте никогó, ктó бы то ни́ был.
Don't let anyone in, no matter who it is.

Во чтó бы то ни стáло.
Regardless, come what may.

CONDITIONALS

§116 Conditionals are statements not of fact but of possibility. One must distinguish between two types of conditionals: OPEN conditionals and UNFULFILLED conditionals.

(i) An open conditional statement is within the realm of possibility; the action expressed in the main clause can be carried out.

(ii) An unfulfilled conditional statement is contrary to fact and is such that the action was not, or cannot be, carried out.

§117 OPEN CONDITIONALS

Éсли вы прочитáли э́ту кни́гу, дáйте её мне.
If you have read the book, give it to me.

Пойди́те посмотрéть э́ту пьéсу, éсли у вас бýдет врéмя.
Go and see this play if you have time.

Éсли хóчешь, чтóбы дéло бы́ло сдéлано хорошó, дéлай егó сам.
If you want a thing well done, do it yourself.

If the statement as a whole refers to the future, the verb in the subordinate clause (éсли ..., когдá ...) is also in the future:

Приходи́те, éсли (когдá) вы бýдете в гóроде.
Please call if (when) you are in town.

Я придý, éсли я не бýду сли́шком зáнят.
I shall come unless (if ... not) I am too busy.

Éсли (когдá) мы бýдем жить в Лóндоне, мы бýдем ходи́ть в теáтр как мóжно чáще.
If (when) we live in London, we shall go to the theatre as often as possible.

91

§118 UNFULFILLED CONDITIONALS

Бы and the past tense are used in both the main and the conditional clauses; it normally follows immediately after **если**:

Если бы я прочитáл кнѝгу, я вам дал бы её.
If I had read the book, I would give (have given) it to you.

Если бы вы жѝли в Лóндоне, вы моглѝ бы ходѝть в теáтр чáсто.
If you lived (had lived) in London, you could often go (have gone) to the theatre.

Бы́ло бы хорошó, éсли бы мы моглѝ встречáться почáще.
It would be (would have been) nice, if we could meet (could have met) more often.

Если бýдет хорóшая погóда, мы поéдем в воскресéнье зá город.
If it is fine on Sunday, we shall go into the country.

Если бы былá хорóшая погóда, мы поéхали бы в воскресéнье зá город.
If it had been fine on Sunday, we would have gone into the country.

Если бы я знал, что бýдет (see §87) хорóшая погóда, мы поéхали бы в воскресéнье зá город.
If I knew (had known) that it was going to be fine on Sunday, we would go (would have gone) into the country.

NOTE. The word **éсли** is sometimes omitted in colloquial speech:
Бýдет врéмя, я зайдý к вам на часóк.
If I have time, I will call on you for an hour or so.
Бы́ло бы врéмя, я зашёл бы к вам на часóк.
Had there been time I would have called on you for an hour or so.

§119 **Если** is used with the infinitive in statements of a generalising nature:

Если идтѝ (вы пойдёте) прямо, вы вы́йдете к стáнции Метрó.
If you walk straight ahead you will come to the Metro station.

Если бы посмотрéть (вы посмотрéли) бóлее пристáльно, то бы́ло бы замéтно . . .
If one were to look more closely, one would notice . . .

NOTE. The idiomatic use of the imperative in a conditional sense should be used with caution:
Опоздáй он хоть на минýту, все бы погѝбли.
Had he come a moment later, all would have been lost.
Бывáют встрéчи, котóрые не забýдутся, **прожѝви** ты хоть сто лет. [Б. Полевóй]
There are encounters which can never be forgotten, if one were to live a hundred years.

TRANSLATION OF 'TO BE'

§120 In normal use **быть** as a link verb is omitted in the present but expressed in the past and future:

Мой брат до́ма.	*My brother is at home.*
Мой брат — инжене́р.	*My brother is an engineer.*
Мой брат был до́ма.	*My brother was at home.*
Мой брат бу́дет инжене́ром.	*My brother is going to be an engineer.*

Есть is used emphatically to translate *is, exists* (see also §123):

Есть (был) тако́й челове́к.	*Yes, there is (was) such a person.*
Нет (не́ было) тако́го челове́ка.	*No, there is (was) no such person.*

For the use of **нет**, see §141.

§121 THERE IS, THERE ARE

Sentences of the type: *There are several new pupils in the class, there are many new books here*, are rendered by inversion, the sentence starting with the adverb or adverbial phrase:

В кла́ссе не́сколько но́вых ученико́в, здесь мно́го но́вых книг.

If the sentence contains no such adverb or phrase, inversion is impossible and **есть** is used:

Есть не́сколько но́вых ученико́в.	*There are several new pupils.*
Есть мно́го но́вых книг.	*There are many new books.*

§122 *To be* is often rendered by verbs that are more precise or more evocative than **быть**:

(i) Кни́га **лежи́т** на столе́.   *The book is on the table.*

На стене́ **виси́т** карти́на.   *There is a picture on the wall.*

В углу́ **стоя́ла** больша́я крова́ть.
There was a large bed in the corner.

В га́вани **стоя́ли** три корабля́.
There were three ships in the harbour.

Гости́ница **нахо́дится (располо́жена)** недалеко́ от па́рка.
The hotel is near a park.

Ло́ндон **нахо́дится (располо́жен, лежи́т)** на реке́ Те́мзе.
London is on the River Thames.

Вдали **тяну́лся** (**простира́лся, видне́лся, темне́л, шёл**) огро́мный лес.

There was a huge forest in the distance.

Вблизи **протека́ет** река́.   *There is a river nearby.*

Неда́вно в Ло́ндоне **состоя́лся** большо́й кри́кетный матч.

There was a big cricket match in London recently.

(На трибу́нах) **собрало́сь** пятьдеся́т ты́сяч зри́телей.

There was a crowd of fifty thousand (on the stands).

Раздали́сь бу́рные аплодисме́нты.   *There was stormy applause.*

С холма́ **открыва́лся** хоро́ший вид.

There was (we had) a good view from the hill.

Кремль **представля́ет собо́й** великоле́пный вид.

The Kremlin is a splendid sight.

Глубо́кое молча́ние **цари́ло** вокру́г.

There was deep silence all around.

Стоя́ла прекра́сная пого́да.

The weather was beautiful.

(ii) **Ока́зываться/оказа́ться** is used more commonly than its English equivalent *turn out to be*. It often translates *to be* when a change in circumstances or an element of surprise is implied:

По́сле сме́рти отца́ дела́ оказа́лись тру́дными.

After the death of his father things were difficult.

Он оказа́лся в тру́дном положе́нии.

He was in a difficult position.

Очути́ться (*pfv.*) is used in a similar sense, *to be*, *find oneself*:

Мы очути́лись (оказа́лись) в незнако́мом ме́сте.

We were (found ourselves) in a strange place.

Note that **находи́ться** seldom translates *to find oneself*; see above, §122(i).

§123 Есть, — э́то, — вот and **явля́ться** are often used in definitions and abstract statements:

Сове́тский Сою́з есть многонациона́льное госуда́рство.

The Soviet Union is a multi-national state.

Свобо́да — (э́то) ве́чная цель челове́чества.

Liberty is Man's eternal goal.

94

Со́лнце явля́ется приро́дным исто́чником эне́ргии.
The sun is a natural source of energy.

See also §31.

§124 Быва́ть/побыва́ть. Its main uses are:

(i) As a frequentative (*I usually am, tend to be*):

По вечера́м я всегда́ быва́ю до́ма.
I am always at home in the evenings.

Ра́нним ле́том пого́да быва́ет хоро́шая.
The weather is usually fine in early summer.

Уро́ки быва́ют три ра́за в неде́лю.
There are three lessons a week.

Уста́лые лю́ди быва́ют раздражи́тельными.
Tired people tend to be irritable.

(ii) To stress intermittency:

Иногда́ переда́чи быва́ют таки́е ску́чные, что про́сто не сто́ит слу́шать.
Sometimes the programmes are so dull that it is just not worth listening.

У вас есть ру́сские газе́ты? — Быва́ют, коне́чно, но не ка́ждый день.
Have you any Russian newspapers? We do get them, of course, though not every day.

Быва́ют слу́чаи, когда́...   *There are occasions when...*

(iii) To express *go, visit*:

Зимо́й он ча́сто быва́ет в теа́тре (=ча́сто хо́дит в теа́тр).
He often goes to the theatre in winter.

Ра́ньше он быва́л у нас ча́ще (=приходи́л к нам ча́ще).
He used to visit us more frequently.

Кто побыва́л в Швейца́рии и А́встрии, (тот) никогда́ не забу́дет красоту́ гор.
Anyone who has ever been to Switzerland and Austria will never forget the beauty of the mountains.

NOTE. Быть and быва́ть, when thus virtually fulfilling the functions of verbs of motion (cf. §128), are nonetheless followed by в, на +*prep.* and у +*gen.* Nor is the genitive construction used in negative statements.

Я был у ва́шего бра́та.   *I have been to your brother's place.*
Она́ не быва́ла в Ки́еве.   *She has never been to Kiev.*

(iv) To render *does not happen, exist,* etc.:

Таки́х веще́й не быва́ет.
Such things just do not happen.

Никогда́ не быва́ло таки́х люде́й.
Such persons have never existed.

§125 Быва́ло is used parenthetically to express occurrences at irregular intervals (*there were times when . . .*). It is used with both the present and past imperfective and the future perfective:

Я занима́юсь (занима́лся), быва́ло, споко́йно у себя́ в ко́мнате, а сосе́д захо́дит (зайдёт) поболта́ть.
I would be working quietly in my room and my neighbour would call to have a chat.

В мо́лодости он, быва́ло, броди́л по гора́м и доли́нам оди́н.
In his youth he would roam on his own over hills and valleys.

Быва́ло, пройдёт дождь, тогда́ ско́лько поя́вится грибо́в.
When it stopped raining, there used to be ever so many (lit. *how many*) *mushrooms.*

Note the expression **как ни в чём не быва́ло**, *as calmly as you like,* etc.:

Хотя́ бы́ло я́сно, что ему́ бо́льно от ра́ны, он шути́л как ни в чём не быва́ло.
Although the wound was obviously hurting him, he joked as if there was nothing to it.

§126 (i) Бы́ло used parenthetically in conjunction with past perfective verbs (or with **хоте́ть — хоте́л бы́ло**, *intended, tried*) means *I was just on the point of* and implies that the action was not carried out or at least ended soon after it began:

Я вы́шел бы́ло на у́лицу, но шёл дождь, и я верну́лся в дом.
I was just going out, but it was raining and I went back indoors.

Он хоте́л бы́ло пройти́ ми́мо, но она́ останови́ла его́.
He was going to pass her, but she stopped him.

(ii) **Собира́ться/собра́ться** + *infin.* means *to be about to, to be going to*, without implying that the action was not carried out:

Когда́ Ива́н пришёл, мы уже́ собира́лись вы́йти.
When Ivan came, we were already preparing to go out.

Ми́тя собира́ется поступи́ть в университе́т.
Mitya is going to (preparing to) go to the university.

96

VERBS OF MOTION

I. SIMPLE VERBS

§127 It is important to remember that each of these verbs has THREE forms: TWO imperfectives and ONE perfective in common use; e.g. ходи́ть—идти́/пойти́, *to go* (*on foot*). See the table on page 98.

§128 Forms in column A (abstract, general, unspecified) of the ходи́ть type are used for:

(i) General statements of the type:

Челове́к хо́дит, пти́цы лета́ют, ры́бы пла́вают.
Man walks, birds fly, fishes swim.

Моя́ ма́ленькая до́чка уже́ хо́дит (уме́ет ходи́ть).
My little daughter can already walk.

(ii) Habitual action:

Мой брат хо́дит ка́ждый день в шко́лу.
My brother goes to school every day.

Ле́том мы обы́чно е́здим за грани́цу.
In summer we usually go abroad.

Врач запрети́л ему́ мно́го ходи́ть.
The doctor forbade him to do much walking.

Он но́сит очки́.   *He wears glasses.*

(iii) Movement where motion is not in one fixed direction:

Де́ти бе́гали по двору́.   *The children were running about in the yard.*

Мы ходи́ли по ко́мнатам.   *We went from room to room.*

Он ходи́л взад и вперёд по ко́мнате.   *He paced the room.*

(iv) A single, complete action, going and returning ('round trip'), IN THE PAST TENSE ONLY; the actual journeys are not emphasized:

Вчера́ мы с бра́том ходи́ли (е́здили) в го́род (= бы́ли в го́роде).
Yesterday my brother and I went to town.

В про́шлом году́ мы е́здили во Фра́нцию (= бы́ли во Фра́нции).
We went to France last year.

Она́ ходи́ла (е́здила) за до́ктором.
She fetched the doctor.

Cf. §§98, 124(iii).

	Imperfective		Perfective
	A (abstract)	B (concrete)	

Section 1
to go (*on foot*)

	ходи́ть (хожу́, хо́дишь)	идти́ (иду́, идёшь; шёл, шла)	пойти́ (пойду́, пойдёшь; пошёл, пошла́)

to lead (*take*)

	води́ть (вожу́, во́дишь)	вести́ (веду́, ведёшь; вёл, вела́)	повести́ (поведу́, поведёшь; повёл, повела́)

to carry (*take*)

	носи́ть (ношу́, но́сишь)	нести́ (несу́, несёшь; нёс, несла́)	понести́ (понесу́, понесёшь; понёс, понесла́)

Section 2
to go (*by vehicle*)

	е́здить (е́зжу, е́здишь)	е́хать (е́ду, е́дешь; е́хал, е́хала)	пое́хать (пое́ду, пое́дешь; пое́хал, пое́хала)

to transport (*take*)

	вози́ть (вожу́, во́зишь)	везти́ (везу́, везёшь; вёз, везла́)	повезти́ (повезу́, повезёшь; повёз, повезла́)

Section 3
Others include:
to run

	бе́гать (бе́гаю, бе́гаешь)	бежа́ть (бегу́, бежи́шь . . . бегу́т; бежа́л, бежа́ла)	побежа́ть (побегу́, побежи́шь . . . побегу́т; побежа́л, побежа́ла)

to swim, float, sail

	пла́вать (пла́ваю, пла́ваешь)	плыть (плыву́, плывёшь; плыл, плыла́)	поплы́ть (поплыву́, поплывёшь; поплы́л, поплыла́)

to fly

	лета́ть (лета́ю, лета́ешь)	лете́ть (лечу́, лети́шь; летёл, летёла)	полете́ть (полечу́, полети́шь; полетёл, полетёла)

to climb

	ла́зить (ла́жу, ла́зишь)	лезть (ле́зу, ле́зешь; лез, ле́зла)	поле́зть (поле́зу, поле́зешь; поле́з, поле́зла)

NOTE. Both columns A and B are imperfective. Their respective functions are given in §§ 128-9.

§129 Forms in column B (concrete, specific) of the **идти** type are used:

(i) To describe a particular journey in progress, being in one direction only. The direction is either stated or may be implied:

Я шёл (ехал) в город, когда я встретил его.
I was going (was on my way) to town when I met him.

Куда вы идёте (едете)? — Я иду (еду) в город.
Where are you going? I am going to town.

Он шёл по улице, напевая песню. (ходил = *walked up and down*)
He went along the street, humming a tune.

Мы уже шли больше часа.
We had already walked for over an hour.

Самолёт летел высоко над городом. (летал = *circled over*)
The aeroplane flew high above the town.

Мальчики лезли на крутую скалу.
The boys climbed a steep cliff.

Note the conversational use of the present tense of **идти** and **ехать** with a future meaning:

Сегодня вечером я иду в кино.
I am going to the cinema tonight.

В будущем году мы едем во Францию.
We are going to France next year.

(ii) In certain cases the 'concrete' verb is used even to describe repeated action. This applies when the movement is clearly in one direction only, the time of the occurrence often confirming this:

Каждое утро я **иду** мимо вашего дома на работу.
I pass your house every morning on my way to work.

but:

Я **хожу** на работу каждый день (= я бываю на работе каждый день). (See §124, iii.)

I walk to work every day (both journeys and the time spent at work being understood).

В шесть часов они вставали, **шли** на поля на работу и там оставались до позднего вечера.

They got up at 6 a.m., went to work in the fields and stayed there till late in the evening.

99

Зимóй мы идём (ложи́мся) спать в дéсять часóв вéчера.
In the winter we go to bed at 10 p.m.

THE USES OF VERBS IN SECTIONS 1 AND 2 (see page 98)

§130 Verbs in section 1 express actions performed on foot, those in section 2 actions by persons travelling in vehicles.

Compare these translations of *the mother is taking the girl to the doctor*:

Мать **ведёт** дéвочку к врачý. (Мать идёт пешкóм, и дéвочка идёт с ней.)

Мать **несёт** дéвочку к врачý. (Мать идёт пешкóм, а дéвочка óчень больнá, или ещё не хóдит, и так прихóдится мáтери нести́ её на рукáх.)

Мать **везёт** дéвочку к врачý. (Мать éдет в маши́не, и дéвочка éдет с ней.)

Also:

В прóшлом годý мы вози́ли бáбушку на мóре (мы éздили на мóре и бáбушка былá с нáми, мы взя́ли её с собóй).
Last year we took our grandmother to the seaside.

éздить–éхать/поéхать пóездом   *to take the train*

See also §196.

§131 **Ходи́ть–идти́/пойти́** is also used of vehicles:

Автóбусы хóдят с рáннего утрá до чáсу нóчи.
Buses run from early morning till 1 a.m.

Пóезд шёл со скóростью семи́десяти киломéтров в час.
The train was travelling at seventy km.p.h.

Парохóд шёл (плыл) не óчень бы́стро.
The steamer was not going very fast.

Éздить–éхать/поéхать is, however, more common with **маши́на, автомоби́ль**, etc.:

Маши́на éхала (шла) по середи́не ýлицы.
The car was travelling along the middle of the road.

but:

Вот идёт егó маши́на.   *Here comes his car.*

To drive a car is водить-вести/повести машину, править (управлять) машиной[1]; *a driver* is водитель, шофёр.

§132 Носить also means *to wear habitually*:

Зимой она носит шляпу и тёплое пальто.
In winter she wears a hat and a warm coat.

Он уже давно носит очки.
He has been wearing spectacles for a long time.

Нести is NOT used in the sense *to be wearing*; see §154.

§133 Further uses of идти/по–, вести/по–, везти/по– (see also §134):

Дождь идёт; зимой часто идут дожди.	*It is raining; it often rains in winter.*
Шёл густой снег.	*It was snowing heavily.*
Весна идёт.	*Spring is coming.*
Время идёт быстро.	*Time flies.*
Мои часы идут правильно.	*My watch is right.*
Письма отсюда в Москву идут шесть-семь дней.	*Letters take six or seven days from here to Moscow.*
На этой неделе идёт интересная пьеса.	*There is an interesting play on this week.*
Это платье ей не идёт.	*This dress does not suit her.*
Его дела идут хорошо.	*His affairs are in a good state.*
Дорога шла лесом.	*The road led through a forest.*
Эта дорога ведёт к станции.	*This road leads to the station.*
вести спокойную жизнь	*to lead a quiet life*
вести хозяйство	*to manage the house*
вести войну	*to wage war*

[1] Гонять-гнать (гоню, гонишь)/погнать means *to drive, chase*:

гнать стадо, гнать лошадей   *drive a herd, urge on the horses*
Ветер гнал тучи по тёмному небу.
The wind drove clouds across the dark sky.

The verb is used colloquially in expressions like:

Шофёр гнал машину сломя голову.
The driver drove the car at breakneck speed.

101

вести себя   *to behave oneself*

Ему везёт (везло, повезло).   *He is (was) lucky.*

With such expressions 'abstract' verbs (column A — **ходить, водить, возить**) CANNOT be used.

§134 The PERFECTIVE aspect is formed from concrete verbs (column B — **идти: пойти; везти: повезти**, etc.) and expresses a single, completed action only, though often with the emphasis on its beginning[1]:

Он пошёл (отправился) домой.   *He went home (set out for home).*

Мы пошли дальше.   *We walked on.*

Дождь пошёл.   *It started to rain.*

Compare the following translations of *he swam as far as the new bridge*:

Он **поплыл** к новому мосту (и вышел из воды).

Он **плавал** к новому мосту (туда и обратно).

Thus, too:

Летом Джим Смит **поехал** в СССР, и теперь он живёт в Киеве.

Летом Джим Смит **ездил** в СССР, а теперь он опять в Англии.

See also §§98, 128.

II. COMPOUND VERBS OF MOTION

§135 These do not have two imperfective forms as the simple verbs of motion do, and are 'normal' verbal pairs. The IMPERFECTIVES are compounded with –**ходить**, –**езжать** (from **ездить**), –**носить**, –**возить**, –**летать**, etc., and the PERFECTIVES with –**йти** (from **идти**), –**ехать**, –**нести**, –**везти**, –**лететь**, etc.:

Он часто заходит (заезжает) к нам.   *He often comes to see us.*

---

[1] The rarer perfectives like **походить** mean *to walk about for a short time*:

Сначала он походил по комнате, затем он сел за стол и начал писать.
At first he walked up and down his room and then he sat down at the table and started writing.

Мы поплавали в реке, затем легли на берегу и скоро заснули.
We swam about in the river for a while, then we lay down on the bank and soon fell asleep.

Он захо́дит/заезжа́ет (зайдёт/зае́дет) к нам за́втра.
He is coming (will come) to see us tomorrow.

Он проходи́л ми́мо на́шего до́ма, когда́ я уви́дел его́.
He was walking past our house when I saw him.

Он уже́ прошёл ми́мо на́шего до́ма, когда́ я уви́дел его́.
He had already passed our house when I saw him.

Он ча́сто прохо́дит ми́мо на́шего до́ма в шко́лу.
He often walks past our house on his way to school.

Он ско́ро пройдёт ми́мо на́шего до́ма.
He will pass our house soon.

Он бу́дет ка́ждый день проходи́ть ми́мо на́шего до́ма в шко́лу.
He will pass our house every day on his way to school.

Some of the more common compound verbs of motion:

enter, come in	входи́ть/войти́ въезжа́ть/въе́хать	в + *acc.*	вход, *entrance* въезд, *entrance*
arrive, come	приходи́ть/прийти́ приезжа́ть/прие́хать	в, на + *acc.* or к + *dat.*	прихо́д, *arrival;* *parish* прие́зд, *arrival*
approach, come up to	подходи́ть/подойти́ подъезжа́ть/подъе́хать	к + *dat.*	подхо́д, *approach* подъе́зд, *drive,* *doorway*
reach, go as far as	доходи́ть/дойти́ доезжа́ть/дое́хать	до + *gen.*	дохо́д, *income*
call on, call for	заходи́ть/зайти́ заезжа́ть/зае́хать	к + *dat.* and за + *instr.*	
go out, leave[1]	выходи́ть/вы́йти выезжа́ть/вы́ехать	из + *gen.*	вы́ход, *exit* вы́езд, *exit, de-* *parture*
go away, leave[1]	уходи́ть/уйти́ уезжа́ть/уе́хать	от + *gen.* из, с + *gen.*	ухо́д, *departure;* за + *instr., care* *(of sick,* etc.) уе́зд, *district*
move away from, depart (of train)[1]	отходи́ть/отойти́ отъезжа́ть/отъе́хать	от + *gen.*	отхо́д, *departure* отъе́зд, *departure*

[1] See §185 (i).

pass	проходи́ть/пройти́ проезжа́ть/прое́хать	ми́мо + *gen.*	прохо́д, *passage* прое́зд, *thorough-fare*
cross cross, move house	переходи́ть/перейти́ переезжа́ть/перее́хать	+ *acc.* or че́рез + *acc.*	перехо́д, *crossing* перее́зд, *crossing, removal*
descend	сходи́ть/сойти́	с + *gen.*	
part, disperse	расходи́ться/разойти́сь разъезжа́ться/разъе́хаться		расхо́д, *expense*
find	находи́ть/найти́	+ *acc.*	нахо́дка, (*lucky*) *find*
Note also: originate, occur	происходи́ть/произойти́	из + *gen.*	происхожде́ние, *origin*
manage without	обходи́ться/обойти́сь	без + *gen.*	

The same use of prefixes and prepositions also applies to verbs like: приноси́ть/принести́, приводи́ть/привести́, привози́ть/привезти́ (*bring*); уноси́ть/унести́, уводи́ть/увести́, увози́ть/увезти́ (*take away*); вбега́ть/вбежа́ть, убега́ть/убежа́ть (*run into, run away*); прилета́ть/прилете́ть (*to arrive by air*); выгоня́ть/вы́гнать (*to drive out*), etc.

§136 STAND, SIT, LIE, PUT, etc.

1	2	3
stand стоя́ть/по–	*go and stand* станови́ться/стать	*put* ста́вить/по–
sit сиде́ть/по–	*sit down* сади́ться/сесть	*put* сажа́ть, сади́ть/посади́ть
lie лежа́ть/по–	*lie down* ложи́ться/лечь	*put, lay* класть/положи́ть

(i) *Note to column* 1: All three verbs are of the second conjugation: **стоя́ть**: стою́, стои́шь; **сиде́ть**: сижу́, сиди́шь;
лежа́ть: лежу́, лежи́шь
and all three perfective aspects are formed with **по–** (see §95, i).
These verbs indicate position; they are followed by **в** or **на** with the PREPOSITIONAL, **под** with the INSTRUMENTAL, etc.

For the use of these verbs as translations of *to be*, see §122(i).

Note to column 2: The imperfective verbs are reflexive and the perfective verbs irregular monosyllabics:

становиться: становлюсь, становишься; становился, становилась; становись! (становитесь!)

стать: стану, станешь; стал, стала; стань(те)!

садиться: сажусь, садишься; садился, садилась; садись! (садитесь!)

сесть: сяду, сядешь ... сядут; сел, села; сядь(те)!

ложиться: ложусь, ложишься; ложился, ложилась; ложись! (ложитесь!)

лечь: лягу, ляжешь ... лягут; лёг, легла; ляг(те)!

These verbs indicate intransitive motion; they are followed by **в, на, под**, etc. with the ACCUSATIVE.

Становиться/стать means:

(*a*) *go and stand*: Станьте сюда! Он стал в очередь.[1]

(*b*) *become*: Он стал доктором. Дни становятся длиннее.

(*c*) *begin* (**стать** only): Он стал читать. Он стал ещё чаще ходить к нам.

Note to column 3:

ставить: ставлю, ставишь; ставь(те)!

класть: кладу, кладёшь; клал, клала; клади(те)!

Сажать/посадить means both *to put* and *to plant*: **сажать цветы, деревья** (cf. **сад**, *garden* and English 'to set').

Note also **совать** (**сую, суёшь**)/**сунуть**, *to put, thrust into*[2]:

Он сунул руку (деньги) в карман.
He put his hand (money) into his pocket.

Он суёт свой нос в чужие дела.
He pokes his nose in other people's business.

These are transitive verbs of motion; they are followed by **в, на, под**, etc. with the ACCUSATIVE.

---

[1] The more common verb corresponding to **садиться/сесть, ложиться/лечь** is **вставать/встать**, *to get up, stand up*:
Когда мы вошли, они все встали.

[2] **Соваться/сунуться** means *to push, butt in, meddle*, etc.:
Вперёд не суйся, назади не оставайся.
Don't get out too far in front and don't be left in the rear.
соваться с советами *to proffer advice* (usually unhelpful and unwanted)

(ii) Compare the use of cases in the following examples:

⌠Я поста́вил зо́нтик в у́гол.	*I put the umbrella in the corner.*
⌡Он стои́т в углу́.	*It is standing in the corner.*
⌠Я положи́л кни́гу на стол.	*I put the book on the table.*
⌡Она́ лежи́т на столе́.	*It is lying on the table.*
⌠Я посади́л де́вочку на стул.	*I put the little girl on the chair.*
⌡Она́ сиди́т на сту́ле.	*She is sitting on the chair.*
⌠Я лёг на посте́ль.	*I lay down on my bed.*
⌡Я лежу́ на посте́ли.	*I am lying on my bed.*
⌠Я сел на стул.	*I sat down on the chair.*
⌡Я сижу́ на сту́ле.	*I am sitting on the chair.*
⌠Я стал в о́чередь.	*I went to stand (stood) in the queue.*
⌡Я стою́ в о́череди.	*I am standing in the queue.*

Note, however, the use of the prepositional in the following where movement into the room, bed, etc., is not implied:

Че́рез не́которое вре́мя меня́ попроси́ли сесть в приёмной.
After a while, I was asked to take a seat in the waiting-room.

Ребёнок сел в посте́ли.   *The child sat up in bed.*

Мы посади́ли в саду́ дере́вья и цветы́.
We planted some trees and flowers in the garden.

Он лёг на полу́ (as opposed to **он лёг на́ пол**) implies that he remained there for a long time, e.g. **и там и лежа́л вплоть до утра́.** The prepositional is also regularly used with **уса́живаться/усе́сться, *to settle down*:

Он вошёл в ко́мнату и усе́лся в удо́бном кре́сле.	*He entered the room and settled down in a comfortable armchair.*

Note the following expressions:

класть/положи́ть в чай са́хару	*to put sugar in (add to) one's tea*
лежа́ть/по– в больни́це	*to be in hospital*
сажа́ть/посади́ть кого́-нибудь в тюрьму́	*to put someone in prison*
сиде́ть/по– в тюрьме́	*to be in prison*
положи́ть чему́-нибудь коне́ц	*to put an end to something*
ложи́ться/лечь в осно́ву (+ *gen.*)	*to form the basis of*

Ложи́ться/лечь is used in descriptions, e.g.

Тума́н ложи́лся на зе́млю.　*A mist settled over the countryside.*

IMPERSONAL EXPRESSIONS

§137 Expressions consisting of the short form of the neuter adjective and the neuter singular form of **быть** (in the past and future only) state weather conditions and general circumstances:

Тепло́ (хо́лодно, светло́, темно́). *It is warm (cold, light, dark).*

Бы́ло тепло́ (бы́ло хо́лодно, бы́ло светло́, бы́ло темно́). *It was warm (cold, light, dark).*

Там (бы́ло) о́чень хорошо́.　　*It is (was) very nice there.*

На у́лицах бы́ло темно́ и ти́хо.　*The roads were dark and silent.*

The person concerned is in the dative:

Мне тепло́ (мне хо́лодно, нам бы́ло те́сно и т. д.). *I am warm (I am cold, we were crowded, etc.).*

Note also: **темне́ет (темне́ло/с–), светае́т (света́ло/рассвело́)**, *it is growing dark, growing light,* etc.

The short form of the neuter adjective is also used with states of mind:

Мне ве́село (гру́стно).[1]　　*I am cheerful (sad).*

Мне ста́ло веселе́е (грустне́е).　*I felt more cheerful (sadder).*

Мне жаль (жа́лко) ва́шего отца́ (ва́шу мать). (See §143, Note.) *I feel sorry for your father (mother).*

Мне ста́ло жа́лко его́.　　　*I felt sorry for him.*

Мне ску́чно.　　　　　　*I am bored, lonely.*

Мне стра́шно.　　　　　*I am frightened.*

Мне ста́ло лу́чше.　　　　*I started feeling better.*

See also §180.

§138 Other impersonal verbs, particularly reflexives, used in constructions with the dative include:

Мне хо́чется (хоте́лось/захоте́лось, захо́чется) пойти́ погуля́ть. *I feel like (felt like, will feel like) going for a walk.*

---

[1] **Он весёлый (он гру́стный)** would mean *he is of a cheerful (melancholy) disposition.*

The personal pronoun is, in fact, often omitted:

| (Мне) не спи́тся. | *I can't get to sleep.* |
| (Мне) не ве́рится. | *I can't believe it.* |

Хоте́лось бы сде́лать э́то самому́.
I'd like to do that myself.

The difference between **я хочу́** and **мне хо́чется** is roughly that between *I want* and *I feel like*. **Мне ве́рится** is a less confident assertion than **я ве́рю**.

For **каза́ться**, see §172; for **нра́виться**, see §186; for **на́до, ну́жно, прихо́дится**, see §189.

§139 Other impersonal expressions are formed by using the 3rd person plural without **они́** (e.g. **говоря́т**, *it is said*). The 3rd person plural is also used to render passives of the type *he is said to be, I was given, I was told*: **о нём говоря́т, что . . . ; мне да́ли; мне сказа́ли**. Note also **так не говоря́т**, *you don't say it like that.* See also §111.

§140 *One, you* (*impers.*) may be translated (i) by the 2nd person singular without **ты**, (ii) by expressions with **мо́жно, нельзя́**, etc., (iii) by **кто́-нибудь**:

Не поймёшь (*fut.pfv.*) ни сло́ва из того́, что он говори́т.
You cannot understand a word of what he is saying.

Если бы кто́-нибудь спроси́л его́, что́ он де́лает, он не знал бы, что́ сказа́ть.
If one were to ask him what he was doing, he would not know what to say.

Мо́жно (нельзя́) писа́ть э́то сло́во так (see §176, ii).
You can (cannot) spell this word like that.

The Negative

§141 USE OF нет, не́ было, не бу́дет

Нет should be regarded as a verb meaning *there is not* and its use indicates that the whole statement is unequivocally negative. The logical subject is in the genitive and the verb is always impersonal (i.e. 3rd person, singular, neuter) regardless of the number and gender of the logical subject:

Его́ нет (=его́ не ста́ло). *He is no more.*

Его́ нет (до́ма). *He is not in.*

Учи́теля (учи́тельницы) нет.
The teacher is not there (there is no teacher).

Учи́теля (учи́тельницы) не́ было.
The teacher was not there (there was no teacher).

Учи́теля (учи́тельницы) не бу́дет.
The teacher will not be there (there will be no teacher).

Contrast the above examples with statements of the type:

Он не учи́тель. *He is not a teacher.*

Он не́ был учи́телем. *He was not a teacher.*

Он не бу́дет учи́телем. *He will not be a teacher.*

where only the second half of the sentence, the predicate, is negated.

Compare:

Мой друг не ру́сский.
My friend is not a Russian.

Моего́ ру́сского дру́га здесь нет.
My Russian friend is not here.

Никако́й до́ктор здесь не помо́жет.
No doctor can help here.

Никако́й наде́жды нет.
There is no hope.

Теа́тр у нас в го́роде не большо́й.
The theatre in our town is not large.

У нас в го́роде нет теа́тра.
In our town there is no theatre.

Similarly, in statements of the type *he is not at home, but at work* it is not the whole statement that is negative, but merely one part of the predicate; therefore, **он не до́ма, а на рабо́те.**

I have not is **у меня́ нет** + *gen.*

У меня́ брат.	У меня́ нет бра́та.
У меня́ был брат.	У меня́ не́ было бра́та.
У меня́ сестра́.	У меня́ нет сестры́.
У меня́ бу́дет вре́мя.	У меня́ не бу́дет вре́мени.

THE GENITIVE AFTER NEGATIVE TRANSITIVE VERBS

§142 It is a fundamental rule that the direct object after a negative transitive verb is expressed in the genitive:

Я ви́дел Кремль.	*I saw the Kremlin.*
Я не ви́дел Кремля́.	*I did not see the Kremlin.*
Я получи́л письмо́.	*I received the letter.*
Я не получи́л письма́.	*I did not receive the letter.*

Ва́ня не принёс пера́ (очко́в, де́нег).
Vanya did not bring his pen (spectacles, money).

Она́ сиде́ла, не поднима́я (подня́в) головы́.
She sat without raising her head.

This applies in particular when multiple negatives are used:

Студе́нты не по́няли ни сло́ва.
The students did not understand a word.

Я не встреча́л ни одно́й ру́сской де́вушки.
I did not meet a single Russian girl.

Он никому́ не доверя́л свое́й та́йны.
He would not confide his secret to anyone.

Он не чита́л никако́й (ни одно́й) кни́ги по-ру́сски.
He has not read any book in Russian.

§143 However, when the object is particularised, the accusative is commonly used, especially with feminine nouns:

Я не понима́ю э́то сло́во.   *I do not understand this word.*

Я не зна́ю Га́лю.[1]	*I do not know Galya.*
Он не чита́л э́ту кни́гу.	*He has not read this book.*
Он не мог подня́ть ле́вую ру́ку от бо́ли.	*He could not raise his left arm because of the pain.*

The accusative is used when the object is followed by an extension:

Я не нахожу́ э́ту кни́гу интере́сной (cf. §45).
I do not find this book interesting.

Я ещё не чита́л кни́гу, кото́рую вы мне да́ли.
I have not yet read the book that you lent me.

The accusative of feminine nouns is very commonly used after negative verbs even in broad generalisations:

Я не ем ры́бу.	*I don't eat fish.*
Он не лю́бит му́зыку.	*He does not like music.*

but:

Я не ем мя́са.	*I don't eat meat.*
Он не лю́бит шу́ма.	*He does not like noise.*

NOTE. A similar tendency to use both the genitive and accusative is found even with certain positive verbs:

Я жду авто́буса.	*I am waiting for a bus.*
Я жду авто́бус.	*I am waiting for the bus.*
Мне жаль ма́му.	*I am sorry for Mother.*
Мне жаль па́пу (отца́).	*I feel sorry for Father.*
Мне ста́ло жаль де́нег.	*I regretted I had spent the money.*

§144 Note the use of the accusative in:

Я пью чай, я не пью чай.	*I drink tea, I don't drink tea.*
but:	
Я не пью кита́йского ча́я.	*I don't drink China tea.*

However, phrases of the type **принима́ть/приня́ть ме́ры**, *to take steps*; **производи́ть/произвести́ впечатле́ние**, *to make an impression*; **обраща́ть/обрати́ть внима́ние**, *to pay attention*, conform to the negative (genitive) construction:

[1] **Я никако́й Га́ли не зна́ю** would mean *I don't know anyone called Galya.*

Они не обращали на нас внимания.

They did not pay any attention to us.

Он не произвёл хорошего впечатления.

He did not make a good impression.

§145 The tendency to use the accusative in certain negative statements does not of course apply to animate masculine nouns (singular and plural) and animate feminine nouns (plural only), where the accusative is in any case identical with the genitive:

Я (не) встречал Ивана (этого человека, этих людей).

I have (not) met Ivan (this person, these persons).

Я (не) видел Катю (эту девушку) в институте.

I saw (did not see) Katya (this girl) at the Institute.

Я (не) видел этих девушек в институте.

I saw (did not see) these girls at the Institute.

See also §21.

§146 POSITION OF **не**

Normally **не** immediately precedes the verb:

Мы не идём в кино; мой брат не изучал немецкого языка.

When however it is not the verb, but another element in the sentence that is negated, **не** is moved accordingly:

Мы идём не в кино, а в театр; мой брат изучал не немецкий язык, а русский.

Compare:

Он этого не сделал.	*He did not do it.*
Не он это сделал.	*It was not he that did it.*
Я не понял ни слова.	*I did not understand a word.*

Я понял не всё, что он говорил.

I did not understand all he said (i.e. I understood what he said, but not everything).

Я не могу прийти.

I cannot come.

Я могу не прийти, если неудобно.

I can stay away, if that would be better (i.e. I won't come, if it is inconvenient).

Не суйся не в своё дело.   *Don't interfere in other people's affairs.*

112

§147 USE OF да AND нет AFTER A NEGATIVE QUESTION

Common usage is as follows:

Вы не англичанин?	*Aren't you English?*
Нет, англичанин.	*Yes, I am.* (Lit. *On the contrary, I AM English.*)
Да, я не англичанин.	*No, I am not.* (Lit. *That's right, I am NOT English.*)
Вы не хотите посмотреть этот фильм?	*Don't you want to see this film?*
Нет, хочу.	*Yes, I do.*
Да, не хочу.	*No, I don't.*

Thus, if the reply is in the negative, as anticipated in the question, да is used; if the reply does not bear out this supposition and is positive, нет is used.

NEGATIVE PRONOUNS, ADJECTIVES AND ADVERBS

§148 A negative statement is incomplete unless it contains the negative particle не or the negative 'verbs' нет and нельзя (see §176, ii), even when it contains such negative words as никто, ничего, никакой, никогда, ни ... ни, etc.:

У него никогда не было денег.	*He never had any money.*
Ничего не было видно.	*We could not see anything.*
Никто не знал об этом.	*Nobody knew about this.*
У них никаких затруднений не было.	*They did not have any (had no) difficulties.*
Он не сказал ни слова.	*He did not say a word.*
Я никогда не был (бывал) в Крыму.	*I have never been to the Crimea.*
Они никогда никуда не ходили.	*They never went anywhere.*
Ни Катя ни Вася не писали сочинения.	*Neither Katya nor Vasya wrote a composition.*

For the use of некому, некуда, etc., see §150.

§149 Note the position of the preposition 'sandwiched' between the two parts of compound negatives:

Ни у когó нé было дéнег.
Nobody had any money.

Дéвушка ни с кéм не говорúла.
The girl did not talk to anybody.

Онú ни на когó не обращáли ни малéйшего внимáния.
They did not pay the slightest attention to anyone.

Дóлгое врéмя мы ни о чём не говорúли.
For a long time we did not talk about anything.

NOTE:

ни за чтó, ни в кóем слýчае
on no account

ни при какúх услóвиях
under no circumstances

§150 The dative and infinitive construction is found in both positive and negative statements:

Что мне дéлать?
What am I to do?

Кудá мне (= кудá я могý) садúться?
Where can I sit?

Посторóнним не (= нельзя́) входúть.
No admittance for unauthorised persons.

Не дойтú мне (= не могý я дойтú) до тебя́.
There is no way for me to reach you.

This construction is common in the negative with **нéкого, нé с кем, нéкогда**, etc. It consists of: the negative word, the impersonal form of **быть**, the infinitive, and the person concerned in the dative (often omitted). **Не** is NOT expressed separately. These statements answer a potential rather than concrete question.

Compare:

CONCRETE

Что онá éла?	*What did she eat?*
Онá ничегó не éла.	*She did not eat anything.*

POTENTIAL

Что ей бы́ло есть?
What had she (what was there for her) to eat?

Ей не́чего бы́ло есть.
She had nothing to eat (there was nothing for her to eat).

Де́лать бы́ло не́чего.
There was nothing to do.

but: Ничего́ не поде́лаешь (*coll.*).

There is nothing you can do about it (there is nothing for it).

Де́вушке не́ с кем бы́ло говори́ть.
The girl had no-one to talk to.

Не́ о чем бы́ло говори́ть.
There was nothing to talk about.

NOTE:

Мне не́куда (идти́).	*I have nowhere to go.*
Не́зачем идти́.	*There is no point in going.*
Мне не́когда.	*I have no time.*
От не́чего де́лать.	*To while away the time.*
Не́ за что (after спаси́бо, etc.).	*Don't mention it.*
Не быть войне́.	*There shall be no war.*

Prepositions

§151 FOR

(i) **Для** + *gen.* means *intended for, for the purpose of, for the sake of, to the advantage of, considering it is.* Under certain circumstances the plain dative may be substituted:

Это письмо для вас.	*This letter is for you.*

Compare:

Вот вам письмо.	*Here is a letter for you.*
Он сделает это для вас.	*He will do this for you.*
Русский язык для начинающих.	*Russian for beginners.*
Для Лондона очень жарко.	*It is very hot for London.*
Для своих лет ребёнок мал.	*The child is small for his age.*
Для меня это слишком трудно.	*This is too difficult for me.*

Compare:

Мне трудно ответить на ваш вопрос.	*It is difficult for me to answer your question.*

NOTE:

купе для курящих	*a smoking compartment*
передача для детей	*a children's broadcast*

(ii) **За** + *acc.* means *on account of, in return for, on behalf of, in place of*:

Спасибо за вашу помощь.
Thank you for your help.

Он заплатил два рубля за билет.
He paid two roubles for the ticket.

Все уважают его за его честность.
Everybody respects him for his honesty.

Все голосовали за предложение (против предложения).
Everybody voted for (against) the motion.

Они сражались (умерли) за родину.
They fought (died) for their country.

116

| Óко за óко, зуб зá зуб. | *An eye for an eye, a tooth for a tooth.* |
| Я óчень рад за вас. | *I am so glad for you.* |

Compare:

| Я вам óчень рад. | *I am so glad to see you.* |

NOTE:

| (Я пью) за вáше здорóвье. | (*I drink to*) *your health.* |
| Что за мужчи́на! | *What a man!* |

(iii) **За** + *instr.* means *for* when expressing purpose with verbs of motion, etc.:

Он зашёл за мной.	*He called for me.*
Они́ послáли за пóмощью.	*They sent for help.*
Он стоя́л в óчереди за билéтами.	*He queued for tickets.*

NOTE:

Он ходи́л за дóктором.	*He fetched the doctor.*
Онá пошлá за покýпками.	*She went to do her shopping.*
Онá вы́шла зáмуж за рýсского.	*She married a Russian.*
Онá зáмужем за рýсским.	*She is married to a Russian.*

(iv) **На** + *acc.* often translates *for* (see also Expressions of Time, §163):

билéты на четы́ре мéста	*tickets for four*
кóмната на трёх (человéк)	*a room for three persons*
сдáча на оди́н фунт	*change for one pound* (*sterling*)
надóлго, навсегдá	*for long, for good*
напримéр	*for example*

NOTE:

товáры нá два ши́ллинга	*two shillings' worth*
несмотря́ на всё э́то	*in spite of all this*
наскóлько мне извéстно (я знáю)	*as far as I know*
опáздывать/опоздáть на рабóту на дéсять минýт	*to be ten minutes late for work*

(v) **От** + *gen.* means *for* in the sense *because of, as a result of*:

| Онá заплáкала от рáдости. | *She wept for joy.* |

117

NOTE:

лека́рство (сре́дство) от головно́й бо́ли	*a remedy for headaches*

See also §157.

(vi) **По** + *dat.* means *for* in the sense of *by reason of*:

По како́й причи́не?	*For what reason?*
По той просто́й причи́не, что...	*For the simple reason that ...*
Она́ вы́шла за́муж по любви́.	*She married for love.*

See also §§156, 159.

(vii) Sometimes *for* is translated by the plain genitive:

Он попроси́л по́мощи.	*He asked for help.*
на́ши пла́ны пое́здки во Фра́нцию	*our plans for a trip to France*
причи́на его́ отсу́тствия	*the reason for his absence*

NOTE:

Он уе́хал в Москву́, на Украи́ну.	*He has left for Moscow, for the Ukraine* (see §153).

§152 в (во)[1] +*prep.* or *acc.*, **из (изо)**[1] +*gen.*

(i) IN used with an enclosed space, building, town, country, etc. is generally expressed by **в** +*prep.*:

Что у тебя́ в карма́не?
What have you got in your pocket?

Они́ живу́т в большо́м до́ме (в дере́вне, в Ки́еве, в А́нглии).
They live in a big house (in the country, in Kiev, in England).

---

[1] **Во** is used:

(i) Before **бл–, дв–, мн–, сн–**, e.g. во бла́го, во дворе́, во сне, во мно́гом; but в два часа́, вдвоём.

(ii) Before two consonants if the first is **в** or **ф**, e.g. во-вторы́х, во фли́геле, во Фра́нции, во всём, во вся́ком слу́чае; but в своём до́ме.

(iii) In во-пе́рвых, во главе́, во рту, во что; note also во и́мя; but в кни́ге, в стране́, в сча́стье, в шко́ле.

Изо is used before **вс–** and **дн–**, e.g. изо всех сил, изо дня в день; note also изо рта.

Other examples:

Ко is used before **дн–** ог **мн–**, e.g. ко дню, ко мне, ко мно́гим; but note к дру́гу, к своему́ удивле́нию, к кому́, к го́роду.

Надо is used before **мн–**, e.g. надо мной.

В + *prep.* translates *at* with the following nouns:

в кино́, в шко́ле, в клу́бе, в колхо́зе и т. д.
at the cinema, at school, at the club, at the Collective Farm, etc.

It is also used in an abstract and semi-abstract sense:

В э́том рома́не ничего́ но́вого нет.
There is nothing new in this novel.

В его́ го́лосе слы́шался гнев.	*There was anger in his voice.*
Нет ра́дости в мое́й рабо́те.	*There is no joy in my work.*

Он в хоро́шем (дурно́м) настрое́нии.
He is in a good (bad) mood.

(ii) то, INTO with such expressions is **в** + *acc.*:

Он су́нул де́ньги в карма́н.	*He put the money in his pocket.*
Он идёт в шко́лу (в кино́), он е́дет в Ки́ев (во Фра́нцию).	*He is going to school (to the cinema, to Kiev, to France).*
Он попа́л в дурно́е о́бщество.	*He got into bad company.*

NOTE:

посеще́ние (посети́тель) Ло́ндона	*a visit (visitor) to London*
вход в музе́й	*the entrance to the museum*

(iii) FROM with such expressions is **из** + *gen.*:

Он вы́нул де́ньги из карма́на.	*He took the money from his pocket.*

Он возвраща́ется из шко́лы (из кино́, из Ки́ева, из Фра́нции).
He is returning from school (from the cinema, from Kiev, from France).

цита́та из рома́на	*a quotation from a novel*
из моего́ про́шлого	*from my past*

Обо is used before мн–, вс– or чт–, e.g. обо мне, обо всём (or о всём), обо что. **Об** is used before a vowel, e.g. об э́том, об игре́; note ру́ку о́б руку.

Передо, подо are used before вс– or мн–, e.g. передо все́ми, передо мной; подо все́ми, подо мной.

Со is used:

(i) Before вн–, вс–, вч–, дн–, мн–, e.g. со внима́нием, со все́ми, со вчера́шнего дня, со дня, со мной.

(ii) Often before two consonants if the first is з or с, e.g. со звездо́й, со зна́ком, со свято́й, со сре́дствами, со слу́жбы, со ста́нции; but с зве́рем, с сло́вом, с стиха́ми; note also с кварти́ры, с про́шлого го́да, с собо́й, с тремя́.

119

With the preceding examples, the rule is to express:

POSITION (*in, at*)	by **в** +*prep.*
MOVEMENT TOWARDS (*to, into*)	by **в** + *acc.*
MOVEMENT AWAY FROM (*from, out of*)	by **из** + *gen.*

§153 На +*prep.* or *acc.*; с (со)[1] +*gen.*

(i) ON in its normal sense of *on top* (or *the surface*) *of* is expressed by **на** +*prep.*:

Дом стоя́л на холме́.	*The house stood on a hill.*
Кни́га лежи́т на столе́.	*The book is on the table.*
Карти́на виси́т на стене́.	*The picture is on the wall.*

На +*prep.* is also used:

(*a*) With the following nouns with the sense of *at* or *in*:

заво́д: на заво́де *factory*		ры́нок: на ры́нке	*market*
по́чта: на по́чте *post office*		ро́дина: на ро́дине	*native land*
мо́ре, бе́рег мо́ря: на́ море, на берегу́ мо́ря			*sea, seaside*
пло́щадь: на пло́щади			*square*
вокза́л, ста́нция: на вокза́ле, на ста́нции			*station*
у́лица: на у́лице			*street*
(but переу́лок: в переу́лке *side-street*)			
факульте́т: на факульте́те			*faculty*
ка́федра: на ка́федре			*university department*

(*b*) With nouns indicating functions and activities with the sense *at*[2]:

конце́рт: на конце́рте *concert*		уро́к: на уро́ке	*lesson*
ле́кция: на ле́кции *lecture*		рабо́та: на рабо́те *work*	

(*c*) With certain place-names:

Ура́л: на Ура́ле	*the Urals*
Украи́на: на Украи́не	*the Ukraine*
Кавка́з: на Кавка́зе	*the Caucasus*
Арба́т: на Арба́те	*the Arbat* (district of Moscow)

[1] See §152, footnote 1.

[2] В ле́кции, в конце́рте, etc. would not mean *presence at*, but *in the lecture*, etc. with reference to its content:

В его́ ле́кции бы́ло мно́го интере́сного; в конце́рте был ряд сочине́ний совреме́нных компози́торов.

(*d*) With the points of the compass:

на се́вере (на ю́ге, на восто́ке, на за́паде)
in the north (south, east, west)

(ii) In the kind of expression listed above, то (ON то) is translated by
на + *acc*.:

Она́ подняла́сь на холм.   *She went up the hill.*

Он положи́л кни́гу на стол.   *He put the book on the table.*

Де́ти вы́шли игра́ть на у́лицу.
The children went to play on the street.

Он пое́хал на вокза́л/на ста́нцию (на заво́д/на фа́брику, на ра-
бо́ту, на Украи́ну, на юг).

*He went to the station (to the factory, to work, to the Ukraine, to the
south).*

(iii) FROM is translated by **с (со)** + *gen*. (primary meaning *down from*):

Он сошёл с холма́.   *He came down from the hill.*

Он взял кни́гу со стола́.   *He took the book from the table.*

Он верну́лся с вокза́ла/со ста́нции (с заво́да/с фа́брики, с ра-
бо́ты/со слу́жбы, с уро́ка, с мо́ря/с бе́рега мо́ря, с Украи́ны,
с ю́га).

*He returned from the station (from the factory, from work, from the
lesson, from the seaside, from the Ukraine, from the south).*

With the above, the rule is to express:

POSITION (*on, in, at*)	by **на** + *prep*.
MOVEMENT TOWARDS (*to*)	by **на** + *acc*.
MOVEMENT AWAY FROM (*from, off*)	by **с** + *gen*.

Cf. §152.

§154 Further uses of **в** and **на**:

Они́ игра́ли в кри́кет (в футбо́л, в ка́рты).
They were playing cricket (football, cards).

Он игра́л **на** скри́пке (**на** пиани́но).
He was playing the violin (the piano).

Что бу́дет на обе́д?   *What is there (will there be) for dinner?*

Она́ смотре́ла в окно́.   *She was looking out of the window.*

Она́ постуча́ла в дверь.   *She knocked at the door.*

со слеза́ми **на** глаза́х   *with tears in his eyes*

121

со стра́хом в глаза́х	*with fear in his eyes*

Он был весь в грязи́ (в крови́, в пыли́, в черни́лах). (Cf. §25.)
He was covered in mud (blood, dust, ink).

на со́лнце, на све́жем во́здухе	*in the sun, in the fresh air*
в мо́ре, в откры́том мо́ре	*in the sea, at sea*
на́ море, на берегу́ мо́ря	*at the seaside*
во дворе́	*in the yard*
на дворе́, на у́лице	*outside*
на по́ле	*in (on) the field*
в чи́стом по́ле	*in the open country*
в таку́ю пого́ду	*in such weather*
в э́том отноше́нии	*in this respect*
в слу́чае, е́сли	*in case*
на вся́кий слу́чай	*just in case*
на (са́мом) де́ле	*in fact*
в са́мом де́ле	*in actual fact, really, actually*
в друго́й раз	*some other time*
на друго́й раз, в сле́дующий раз	*next time*

To be wearing is expressed either by в + *prep.* or на + *prep.*:

Он был в чёрной шля́пе и зи́мнем пальто́ or На нём была́
чёрная шля́па и зи́мнее пальто́.[1]
He was wearing a black hat and a winter coat.

§155   AT, TO, FROM

(i) With persons, AT is у + *gen.*, TO (implying movement) к (ко)[2] + *dat.*
and FROM от + *gen.*:

Вчера́ я был у бра́та (у него́).
Yesterday I was at my brother's place (at his place).

Я жил тогда́ у тёти (у неё).
At that time I was living with my aunt, at my aunt's (at her place).

Я иду́ к бра́ту (к нему́).
I am going to see my brother, to my brother's place (to him, to his place).

Незнако́мец подошёл ко мне.
The stranger came up to me.

[1]*Other expressions in common usage include:* он наде́л ('*had put on*') чёрную шля́пу и пальто́: *or* он был оде́т в чёрный костю́м, в зи́мнее пальто́ (*not used of headgear etc.*).

[2] See §152, footnote 1.

Я шёл от брáта (от негó).
I was coming from my brother's place (from his place).

Я получи́л от брáта письмó.
I received a letter from my brother.

(ii) Note these expressions with *from*:

Я взял (óтнял) нож у ребёнка.	*I took the knife from the child.*
Мы знáли по гóрькому óпыту.	*We knew from bitter experience.*
Мнóго людéй ýмерло от стрáшного хóлода.	*Many people died from the terrible cold.*
от стрáха, от бóли	*from fear, from pain*
По егó ви́ду мóжно бы́ло подýмать, что ...	*From his appearance you might suppose that ...*

Note the preposition and case in the following:

Он сел за стол.	*He sat down at the table.*
Он сидéл за столóм.	*He was sitting at the table.*
Он встал из-за столá.	*He rose from the table.*

For *in, at, to, from*, etc. with expressions of time, see §162.

§156 ON, ALONG, etc.

По + *dat.* with verbs of motion expresses *movement along or over the surface of*; **вдоль** + *gen.* means *along, alongside* (both position and movement):

Мы éхали (плы́ли) вниз по Вóлге.
We were travelling down the Volga.

Вдоль по ýлице метéлица метёт. [folk-song]
A snowstorm is sweeping along the street.

Вдоль ýлиц стоя́т высóкие дерéвья.
Tall trees line (lit. *stand along*) *the streets.*

Пó морю плáвали мáленькие кораблú.
Small ships were sailing on the sea.

Он путешéствовал по всемý свéту.
He has travelled all over the world.

Мы ходи́ли по гóроду.
We walked round the town.

For further uses of **по**, see §159.

123

§157 OF

(i) Prepositional phrases formed with *of* are commonly translated by the genitive when expressing possession, relationship, description, content, quantity, etc.:

столи́ца А́нглии	*the capital of England*
произведе́ния Пу́шкина	*the works of Pushkin*
Дворе́ц культу́ры	*Palace of Culture*
челове́к сре́днего ро́ста, недурно́й нару́жности	*a man of medium height, of good appearance*
дни неде́ли	*the days of the week*
стака́н молока́*[1]*	*a glass of milk*

(ii) *Of* is often expressed by an attributive adjective:

Ло́ндонский университе́т	*the University of London*
Азо́вское мо́ре	*the Sea of Azov*
Филологи́ческий факульте́т	*Faculty of Arts*
ночна́я тишина́	*the silence of the night*

(iii) *Of* is omitted in translation when used in appositions (see §32):

го́род Ло́ндон	*the city of London*
село́ Петро́во	*the village of Petrovo*
май ме́сяц	*the month of May*

(iv) *Of*, meaning *concerning*, is translated by **о (об, обо)**[2] +*prep.*:

Мы ду́мали о вас.	*We were thinking of you.*
Я (никогда́) не слыха́л о нём.	*I never heard of him.*

Он дал нам представле́ние о свое́й рабо́те.
He gave us an idea of his work.

but:

основна́я иде́а кни́ги	*the basic idea of the book*

(v) *Of* translated by **от** +*gen.*:

Она́ умерла́ от лихора́дки, от го́лода.	*She died of a fever, of hunger.*

---

[1] Cf. **мешо́к с карто́шкой**, §158. Note also **буты́лка из-под молока́**, *milk bottle*, and **ба́нка из-под варе́нья**, *jam-jar*, which indicate the function, but not necessarily the content, of these receptacles.

[2] See §152, footnote 1.

От до́ма ничего́ не оста́лось.	*Nothing remained of the house.*
ключ от э́той ко́мнаты	*the key of this room*

(vi) *Of* translated by **из** +*gen.*:

три (тро́е) из них, мно́гие из них	*three of them, many of them*

but:

они́ все	*all of them*

гру́ппа из двадцати́ студе́нтов	*a group of twenty students*

but:

гру́ппа студе́нтов	*a group of students*

оди́н из мои́х друзе́й, оди́н. мой друг
a friend of mine

США состои́т из сорока́ девяти́ шта́тов.
The U.S.A. consists of forty-nine states.

костю́м из ше́рсти (сде́ланный из ше́рсти)
a woollen dress (made of wool)

Ничего́ не вы́йдет из э́того.	*Nothing will come of it.*

NOTE:

пье́са Че́хова	*a play by Chekhov*
вход в музе́й	*the entrance of the museum*
вид на ре́ку	*a view of the river*
пое́здка по Москве́	*a tour of Moscow*
Э́то для него́ характе́рно.	*This is characteristic of him.*
Э́то для них типи́чно.	*This is typical of them.*

§158 WITH

(i) **C (co)** +*instr.* describes the person or persons who share in the main action and the circumstances that attend it; the plain instrumental expresses the person by whom or the means by which the action is performed.

Compare:

Он прие́хал с роди́телями.	*He came with his parents.*
Он прие́хал по́ездом.[1]	*He came by train.*

[1] If the noun is qualified by an adjective — *by the early train* — **c** is, however, used: **Он прие́хал с ра́нним по́ездом.**

Он сиде́л за пи́сьменным столо́м с карандашо́м в руке́.
He was sitting at his desk with a pencil in his hand.

Он писа́л карандашо́м.
He was writing with a pencil.

Она́ говори́т гро́мким го́лосом.
She speaks with a loud voice.

Она́ говори́т гро́мким го́лосом и с си́льным акце́нтом.
She speaks with a loud voice and a strong accent.

Он ел мя́со с карто́шкой и овоща́ми.
He was eating meat with potatoes and vegetables.

Он ел мя́со ножо́м и ви́лкой.
He was eating his meat with knife and fork.

Она́ смотре́ла на него́ с больши́м интере́сом.
She looked at him with great interest.

Она́ смотре́ла на него́ испу́ганными глаза́ми.
She looked at him with frightened eyes.

Он вспомина́л о ней с глубо́кой благода́рностью.
He thought of her with deep gratitude.

(ii) **Мы с бра́том**, etc. This type of construction is very common:

мы с отцо́м	*my father and I*
вы с Ива́ном	*you and Ivan*
они́ с сестро́й	*he (she) and his (her) sister*
мы с ва́ми	*you and I*[1]

The verb is generally in the plural, but is in the singular when the second person (or element) is in some way subordinate to the first. Compare:

Мы с сестро́й пое́хали в го́род

and:

Мать с ребёнком пое́хала к врачу́.

The expression is not confined to the subject of the sentence:

У них с жено́й ую́тная кварти́ра.
He and his wife have a pleasant flat.

К нам с бра́том зашли́ друзья́.
Some friends came to see my brother and me.

[1] **Я и брат**, etc. are also used.

(iii) Note these expressions:

Что случи́лось с ва́ми?	*What happened to you?*
мешо́к с карто́шкой[1]	*a sack of potatoes*
хлеб с ма́слом	*bread and butter*
с удово́льствием	*with pleasure*
с быстрото́й мо́лнии	*with lightning speed*
с года́ми	*over the years*
у нас	*with us (at home, in our country)*
Я жил тогда́ у тёти (see also §155).	*I was living with my aunt at that time.*

For further uses of the instrumental, see §§24, 26-31, 44-5, 105-10, 162.

§159 По

(i) **По** + *acc.* means *up to, as far as*:

Он вошёл в во́ду по по́яс.	*He waded into the water up to his waist.*
Я сыт по го́рло.	*I am full up* (lit. *up to my throat*).

(ii) **По** + *dat.* is used after verbs with the distributive prefix **раз–**, *all over, along*:

Они́ разложи́ли кни́ги по всему́ столу́.
They put their books all over the table.

Мно́го истори́ческих городо́в располо́жено по Во́лге.
Many historic cities are situated along the Volga.

По + *dat.* also translates *by* in the following expressions:

по приро́де, по происхожде́нию	*by nature, by origin*
су́дя по его́ ви́ду	*judging by his appearance*
по телефо́ну, по по́чте	*by telephone, by post*
по боле́зни, по оши́бке	*by reason of (through) illness, by mistake*

Other expressions with **по** + *dat.* include:

по его́ сове́ту	*on his advice*
по его́ мне́нию, по-мо́ему	*in his opinion, in my opinion*
по его́ слова́м	*according to him*

[1] Not necessarily a sackful; cf. **стака́н молока́**, §157.

(iii) With verbs like **тосковáть/за–** and **скучáть/соскýчиться**, *to long for*, **по** is normally used with the DATIVE of NOUNS and the PREPOSITIONAL of PRONOUNS:

Онá тоскýет (онá скучáет) по рóдине, по роднóму дóму, по отцý.
She misses her country, her home, her father.

Онá тосковáла (скучáла) по нём.   *She longed for him.*

(iv) **По** + *prep.* also means *on, just after*:

По окончáнии университéта он стал учи́телем.
On leaving the University he became a schoolmaster.

See also §114.

For **по** + *dat.* translating *on, along*, etc. with verbs of motion, see §156; in expressions of time, §162; with distributive numerals, §64.

§160 При + *prep.*

Its main meanings are:

(i) *In the presence of*:

Он сказáл э́то при мне (opposite: без меня́).
He said it in my presence.

при лю́дях	*in public*

(ii) *In the lifetime of, in the reign of*, etc.:

при жи́зни Пýшкина	*during Pushkin's lifetime*
при Петрé Вели́ком	*in the reign of Peter the Great*
при Стáлине	*under Stalin*

(iii) *At, attached to*:

При завóде (имéется) хорóшая столóвая.	*There is a good canteen at the factory.*
при дворé	*at court*

(iv) *For, in spite of*:

При всех егó недостáтках он хорóший человéк.	*For all his faults he is a good man.*
притóм	*moreover*

Note also the following expressions:

ни при каки́х услóвиях	*under no conditions*
при нáшей послéдней встрéче	*at our last meeting*
при пéрвой возмóжности	*at the earliest opportunity*

при одно́м ви́де его́	*merely at the sight of him*
чита́ть при све́те ла́мпы	*to read by lamplight*
при све́те луны́	*in moonlight*
име́ть де́ньги при себе́ (с собо́й)	*to have money on (with) you*
При вхо́де предъяви́ть про́пуск.	*Passes to be shown as you enter.*

EXPRESSIONS OF TIME

§161 THE TIME OF DAY

(i)

Кото́рый час?   *What is the time?*

Час (два часа́, шесть часо́в).
It is one o'clock (two o'clock, six o'clock).

По́лдень (по́лночь).   *It is midday (midnight).*

Полови́на пе́рвого (полови́на тре́тьего, че́тверть двена́дцатого).
It is half past twelve (half past two, quarter past eleven).

одна́ мину́та пе́рвого (пять мину́т шесто́го, два́дцать пять мину́т деся́того)
one minute past twelve (five minutes past five, twenty-five minutes past nine)

без десяти́ три (без пяти́ шесть, без че́тверти оди́ннадцать)
ten to three (five to six, quarter to eleven)

(ii)

В кото́ром часу́? (Во ско́лько? *coll.*)   *At what time?*

в час (в четы́ре часа́, в де́вять часо́в, в полови́ну/полови́не тре́тьего, в че́тверть пя́того)
at one o'clock (at four o'clock, at nine o'clock, at half past two, at a quarter past four)

В is omitted in expressions already containing a preposition:

без десяти́ три	*ten to three* and AT *ten to three*
без че́тверти шесть	*quarter to six* and AT *a quarter to six*

A.m. and *p.m.* are rendered by **утра́, дня, ве́чера, но́чи**:

(в) два часа́ утра́ (но́чи)	(*at*) 2 *a.m.*
(в) де́сять часо́в утра́	(*at*) 10 *a.m.*
(в) три часа́ дня	(*at*) 3 *p.m.*
(в) шесть часо́в ве́чера	(*at*) 6 *p.m.*

129

Note also the following expressions:

ро́вно в во́семь часо́в	*at eight o'clock sharp*
(Уже́) девя́тый час.	*(It is) after eight.*
нача́ло восьмо́го (в нача́ле восьмо́го)	*just after seven*
Го́сти разошли́сь то́лько в пе́рвом часу́ (но́чи).	*The guests only left after midnight.*
к девяти́ часа́м	*by nine o'clock*
к полу́дню (к полу́ночи)	*by midday (midnight)*

§162 IN, ON, AT, FROM (with expressions of time)

Use:

(i) **В** + *acc.* with units of time from a second to a day (see also §164):

В одну́ секу́нду он был по́дле меня́.
In a second he was beside me.

Я ко́нчил свою́ рабо́ту в оди́н час (в оди́н день, в суббо́ту).
I finished my work in one hour (in one day, on Saturday).

в оди́н прекра́сный день	*one fine day*
в сре́ду	*on Wednesday*

(ii) **На** + *prep.* with **неде́ля**, *week*:

на э́той (про́шлой, бу́дущей) неде́ле
this (last, next) week

(iii) **В** + *prep.* with units of time from a month to a century:

В како́м ме́сяце? — В ма́е (ме́сяце).
In which month? In May.

в нача́ле (середи́не, конце́) ма́я
in (at) the beginning (middle, end) of May

В како́м году́? — В ты́сяча девятьсо́т со́рок восьмо́м году́.
In which year? In 1948.

в пе́рвой полови́не двадца́того ве́ка (столе́тия)
in the first half of the twentieth century

в девятна́дцатом ве́ке
in the nineteenth century

Similarly:

в де́тстве, в мо́лодости, в ста́рости
in my (his, etc.) childhood, youth, old age

130

(iv) *From ... to* is **c** + *gen. ...* **до** + *gen.*:

с утра́ до ве́чера	*from morning till evening*
с утра́	*since early morning*

Note also:

изо дня в день	*day after day*
из го́да в год	*year in, year out*

(v) The instrumental is used with the seasons of the year and parts of the day:

весно́й, ле́том, о́сенью, зимо́й	*in spring, summer, autumn, winter*
у́тром, днём, ве́чером, но́чью	*in the morning, afternoon (daytime), evening, night*
сего́дня ве́чером, вчера́ ве́чером	*tonight, last night*
одна́жды ве́чером	*one evening*

Note also:

средь бе́ла дня	*in broad daylight*
среди́ но́чи	*in the middle of the night.*

The instrumental plural expresses protracted, continuous action:

Он рабо́тал це́лыми месяца́ми (подря́д).
He worked for (whole) months on end.

Thus, too, (**це́лыми**) **дня́ми, вечера́ми, ноча́ми, неде́лями, года́ми.**

(vi) **По** + *dat.pl.* is used to express regular recurrence:

по утра́м, по вечера́м, по суббо́там
in the mornings, in the evenings, on Saturdays

§163 FOR (in expressions of time)

(i) Duration of time is expressed by the plain accusative:

Он рабо́тал всё у́тро (всё ле́то).
He worked all morning (all summer).

(ii) The plain accusative translates *for* in such expressions as:

Он рабо́тал два часа́.
He worked for two hours.

Собра́ние продолжа́лось це́лый час.
The meeting went on for a whole hour.

Он гости́л у нас не́сколько дней.
He stayed with us for a few days.

(iii) **На** + *acc.* after verbs of motion translates *for* when it implies *with the intention of staying*:

Мы éдем в Москвý на три недéли.
We are going to Moscow for three weeks.

Compare:

Мы éдем на недéлю.	*We are going for a week.*
Мы éдем (ужé) недéлю.	*We have been travelling for a week.*

Note also:

за послéдние шесть лет[1]	*for the past six years* (see §164)
рабóта на зáвтра	*the work for tomorrow*

§164 FURTHER EXPRESSIONS OF TIME

(i) *Before* is **до** + *gen.*; *just before*, **пéред** + *instr.*, e.g. **до войны́, пéред войнóй**.

(ii) **На** + *acc.* is commonly used when the noun is preceded by an ordinal numeral or **другóй**:

на шестóй день	*on the sixth day*
на трéтий год войны́	*in the third year of the war*
на другóй день	*on the next day*
на другóе ýтро	*next morning*

But in dates (*in* 1960) **в** + *prep.* is used; see §§67, 162(iii).

(iii) **В** + *acc.* is used in the following expressions:

два рáза в день	*twice a day*
во врéмя войны́, в течéние гóда[2]	*during the war, during the year*

---

[1] The difference between **за послéдние шесть лет** and **послéдние шесть лет** is that the former is used of events occurring during the past six years, and the latter of a state of affairs lasting for the entire period:

За послéдние шесть лет он éздил четы́ре рáза в Амéрику, (написáл три нóвых ромáна).

Послéдние шесть лет он жил/живёт в Амéрике, (рабóтал/рабóтает над нóвым ромáном).

[2] The difference between **во врéмя** and **в течéние** is that the former is used with words that are not of an obviously temporal nature (**во врéмя урóка, рабóты, фестивáля**), and the latter, as if to avoid duplication, with temporal expressions (**в течéние чáса, трёх дней, недéли, лéтних мéсяцев**).

(iv) **За** + *acc.* means *during*, especially with the recent past; **в** + *acc.* is used similarly[1]:

за послéднюю недéлю — *during the past week*

за (в) послéдние гóды, за (в) послéднее врéмя (for недáвно, see §84) — *in recent years, recently*

за все эти гóды — *in all these years*

За + *acc.* is also used with **до** + *gen., before*:

за недéлю до егó отъéзда — *a week before his departure*

(v) **Чéрез** + *acc.* is used for *in a week's time, a week later*, etc.:

Я вернýсь чéрез час. — *I'll come back in an hour.*

Он вернýлся чéрез час. — *He came back an hour later.*

Contrast:

Я кóнчу свою рабóту в (за) одúн день.
I'll finish my work in a day.

It is also used with **пóсле** + *gen., after*:

чéрез два дня пóсле начáла семéстра
two days after the beginning of term

[1] See footnote 1 on p. 132.

Conjunctions

§165 AND, BUT

(i) **И** translates *and* in most cases other than those listed below. It is omitted in expressions like *come and see*: **идйте посмотре́ть**. For other occasions when it is omitted, see §7.

(ii) **А** is used when there is a slight contrast between two closely related alternatives; that is, statements which are parallel in meaning or in time:

Взро́слые вы́шли, а де́ти оста́лись до́ма.

The grown-ups went out, and (but, while, whereas) the children stayed at home.

(Мой) брат инжене́р, а сестра́ учи́тельница.

My brother is an engineer and my sister a teacher.

Ленингра́д располо́жен на реке́ Неве́, а Сталингра́д на Во́лге.

Leningrad is on the River Neva and Stalingrad on the Volga.

А is also used in negative statements of the type:

Я не рабо́таю, а чита́ю рома́н.

I am not working but reading a novel.

Мы идём не в теа́тр, а в кино́.

We are not going to the theatre but to the cinema.

Cf. German *sondern*.

(iii) **Но** (*but*) is used when there is a fundamental difference in the nature of the two statements. It makes a more emphatic distinction than **а**:

Здесь о́чень хорошо́, но я не могу́ оста́ться до́льше.

It is very nice here, but I cannot stay any longer.

Рабо́та не о́чень интере́сная, но пла́тят хорошо́.[1]

The job is not very interesting but the pay is good.

(iv) **Но** is also used in apparently contradictory statements:

бе́дная, но счастли́вая, семья́   *a poor but happy family*

---

[1] Неге **но** = **зато́**, *but to make up for that.*

134

Compare:

От Ивáна нет письмá, но надéюсь, что скóро бýдет.
There is no letter from Ivan, but I hope there will be soon.

От Ивáна нет письмá, а (но) от Пáвла есть.
There is no letter from Ivan, but there is one from Pavel.

Письмó не от Ивáна, а от Пáвла.
The letter is not from Ivan but from Pavel.

§166 UNTIL

Until is **покá . . . не** + *fut.pfv.* or *past pfv.*:

Я подождý, покá он не вернётся. *I'll wait till he returns.*

Я подождáл, покá он не вернýлся. *I waited till he returned.*

Я ждал, чтóбы он вернýлся   *I waited for him to return.*
(see §115, iii).

Покá + *impfv.* means *while*, cf. **в то врéмя как**:

Покá Андрéй говорил с отцóм, онá смотрéла в окнó.
While Andrew talked to her father, she looked out of the window.

See also §173.

COMPOUND CONJUNCTIONS

§167 These present some difficulties for the English student, since English syntax is considerably simpler in this respect than Russian. In English a preposition can be used as a conjunction: *after him* (*prp.*), *after he had gone* (*conj.*). This is not the case in Russian. **Пóсле** is a preposition governing the genitive, and requires a noun or pronoun in the genitive. In a compound conjunction this is provided by the demonstrative **то**. The subordinate clause is then introduced by **как**:

пóсле негó
after him

Пóсле **тогó, как** он ушёл, мы все развеселились.
After he had gone, we all cheered up.

Вскóре пóсле **тогó, как** приéхал, он нáчал рабóтать на завóде.
Soon after he arrived, he started to work at the factory.

For the use of gerunds to express such clauses, see §§112-13.

135

§168 Other common prepositions used in forming compound conjunctions include:

(i) **До** + *gen.* and **перед** + *instr.* (*prp.*); **до того, как** and **перед тем, как** (*conj.*):

до обе́да, пе́ред обе́дом, задо́лго до войны́
before dinner, just before dinner, long before the war

До того́, как он уе́хал (как уе́хать) за грани́цу, он рабо́тал в конто́ре.
Before he went abroad he worked in an office.

If *going*, etc. is used or can be substituted for the verb in the subordinate clause (that is, if the subjects of both clauses are the same), an infinitive may be used, i.e. *before going*, **пре́жде чем (пе́ред тем, как; до того́, как) уйти́**:

Пре́жде чем (пе́ред тем, как; до того́, как) уе́хать из го́рода, они́ ещё раз зашли́ ко мне.
Before leaving the town they called on me once more.

Пре́жде чем откры́ть кни́гу, он закури́л папиро́су.
Before opening his book he lit a cigarette.

NOTE:

Он ещё не успе́л отве́тить, как... *Before he had time to answer ...*

(ii) **За** + *acc.* (*prp.*); **за то, что/чтобы** (*conj.*):

Спаси́бо за ва́ше письмо́.   *Thank you for your letter.*

Спаси́бо за то, что вы отве́тили так ско́ро.
Thank you for answering so quickly.

Я за то, чтобы мы сде́лали переры́в.
I'm in favour of making a break.

(iii) **Про́тив** + *gen.*(*prp.*); **про́тив того́, что/чтобы** (*conj.*):

Я про́тив э́того.   *I am against this.*

Я про́тив того́, чтобы вы э́то де́лали.
I am against your doing this.

(iv) **Вме́сто** + *gen.* (*prp.*); **вме́сто того́, чтобы** (*conj.*):

Он пришёл вме́сто бра́та.   *He came in place of his brother.*

Вме́сто того́, чтобы верну́ться домо́й, он провёл ве́чер в го́роде.
Instead of coming home, he spent the evening in town.

(v) **С** + *instr.* (*prp.*); **с тем, что/чтобы** (*conj.*):

Я не согла́сен с ва́ми.   *I do not agree with you.*

Я не согла́сен с тем, что вы говори́те.
I do not agree with what you are saying.

Я э́то де́лаю то́лько с тем (усло́вием), чтобы он продолжа́л
рабо́тать.
I am doing this only on condition that he carries on working.

(vi) Purpose is expressed by **для того́, чтобы; с тем, чтобы**:

Я ей написа́л сра́зу (для того́), чтобы она́ зна́ла, что́ слу-
чи́лось.
I wrote to her at once, so that she should know what had happened.

Я написа́л ей сра́зу (для того́), чтобы дать ей знать, что́ слу-
чи́лось.
I wrote to her at once to tell her what had happened.

For the plain infinitive after verbs of motion, see §115 (iv).

Потому́, что (*orig.* **по тому́, что**); **оттого́ что** (*orig.* **от того́, что**),
because, were formed in the same way. **Несмотря́ на то, что,** *des-
pite the fact that, although,* was originally the gerund of **не смотре́ть,**
followed by **на** + *acc.*

§169 **То** may translate *what, the fact that* (**то, что**), *the way* (**то, как**),
etc.:

То, что вы говори́те, о́чень интере́сно.
What you are saying is very interesting.

Мне нра́вится **то, как** вы расска́зывали э́тот расска́з.
I like the way you told that story.

Я ду́мал **о том, что** мы ви́дели в го́роде.
I was thinking about what we had seen in town.

Мы говори́ли **о том, чтобы** провести́ кани́кулы во Фра́нции.
We were talking about spending our holidays in France.

Мы говори́ли **о том, где** нам провести́ кани́кулы.
We were talking about where to spend our holidays.

Note that in the last two examples the infinitives refer to actions that
have not yet been carried out.

§170 VERBS USED WITH **то**

Note the following examples:

(i) **Добива́ться/доби́ться** + *gen.*, *to achieve*:

Он доби́лся своего́.
He achieved his object.

Он доби́лся того́, что ему́ да́ли лу́чшее ме́сто.
He succeeded in being given a better job.

(ii) **Интересова́ться/за–** + *instr.*, *to be interested*:

Я о́чень интересова́лся ва́шей бесе́дой.
I was very interested in your talk.

Я о́чень интересова́лся тем, что вы расска́зывали.
I was very interested in what you told us.

(iii) **Убежда́ться/убеди́ться в** + *prep.*, *to be convinced*:

Я убеждён в э́том.
I am convinced of this.

Я убеждён в том, что он прав.
I am convinced that he is right.

(iv) **Привыка́ть/привы́кнуть к** + *dat.*, *to become accustomed*:

Он привы́к к вла́сти.
He became accustomed to holding power.

Он привы́к к тому́, чтобы его́ счита́ли вождём.
He became used to being regarded as the leader.

(v) **Начина́ть/нача́ть**, often followed by **с** + *gen.*, *to begin*:

Я не зна́ю, с чего́ мне нача́ть.
I do not know where to start.

Начнём с того́, чтобы прове́рить ва́ше сочине́ние.
Let's start by going over your essay.

Translation of Miscellaneous English Words

§171 ANOTHER

Другой means *another*, in the sense of *different*; **ещё** means *another of the same kind*:

Дайте ещё чашку чаю, пожалуйста; я очень хочу пить.
Give me another cup of tea, please; I am very thirsty.

Дайте мне другую чашку чаю, пожалуйста; этот уже остыл.
Give me another cup of tea, please; this one is cold.

NOTE:

Что будет ещё на обед? — Будет ещё сладкое.
What else is there for dinner? There is also a dessert.

For other uses of **ещё**, see §§53, 173 (Note).

§172 APPEAR, SEEM

(i) *Seems to be, appears to be*, followed by an adjective or noun is translated by **казаться/по-** as the main verb:

Книга казалась интересной.	*The book seemed interesting.*
Он казался старше своих лет.	*He seemed old for his age.*
Он старался казаться оригинальным.	*He tried to appear original.*

(ii) If *seems, appears*, are followed by an infinitive, **кажется (казалось, показалось)** is used parenthetically:

Книга, казалось, интересовала мальчика.
The book seemed to interest the boy.

Он, кажется, ожидает кого-то.
He seems to be expecting someone.

Он, казалось, ничего не знал о нас.
He did not seem to know anything about us.

139

Оказа́лось is more definite:

Оказа́лось, (что) он ничего́ не знал о нас.

It appeared (was clear) that he knew nothing about us.

See also §122(ii).

(iii) This element of conjecture can also be conveyed by **как бу́дто, сло́вно, то́чно**:

Его́ глаза́ как бу́дто напо́лнились невы́плаканными слеза́ми.
[М. Шо́лохов]

His eyes seemed to be filled with unwept tears.

(iv) **Каза́ться/по–** translates *I think, I feel*, in such expressions as:

Кото́рый час? — Ка́жется, пять часо́в.

What is the time?   I think it is five o'clock.

Ка́жется вы уже́ познако́мились?

I think you have already met?

Вдруг мне показа́лось, что всё э́то знако́мо.

I suddenly felt that all this was familiar.

For *to feel*, see also §§137, 180.

(v) **Появля́ться/появи́ться** means *to appear, come into view*:

Она́ появи́лась на балу́ в краси́вом но́вом пла́тье.

She appeared at the dance in a beautiful new dress.

На горизо́нте появи́лось су́дно.

A ship appeared on the horizon.

(vi) **Явля́ться/яви́ться** is similarly used:

Че́рез два дня он яви́лся на рабо́ту.

He appeared (turned up) for work two days later.

For **явля́ться**, *to be*, see §123.

For **вы́глядеть**, *to look, appear*, see §187.

§173 AS

(i) *As, since* (causal) is **так как**:

Так как шёл дождь, я взял зо́нтик.

As it was raining, I took my umbrella.

(ii) *As, when* is **когда́, пока́**, etc.:

Когда́ я вошёл в ко́мнату, она́ подняла́ глаза́.

As I entered the room, she looked up.

140

Когда́ (пока́) мы возвраща́лись домо́й, шёл дождь.
As we returned home, it was raining.

Пока́ идёт дождь, мы остаёмся здесь.
As long as it rains, we are staying here.

(iii) **По ме́ре того́ как** with an imperfective verb translates *as* when two simultaneous processes are described. It sometimes has a meaning similar to **пока́** + *impfv.*, *while*:

По ме́ре того́ как мы приближа́лись к мо́рю, во́здух станови́лся всё прохла́днее.
As we approached the sea, the air became cooler.

По ме́ре того́ как они́ привыка́ли к но́вой жи́зни, они́ забыва́ли о про́шлом.
As they became accustomed to their new life, they forgot about the past.

(iv) *As, like* is **как**:

Де́лайте, как вам ска́зано.
Do as you are told.

Ба́йрон изве́стен как а́втор «Чайльд Гаро́льда».
Byron is known as the author of Childe Harold.

In elliptical comparisons with *as*, *like*, the second element of the comparison is in the nominative:

Я не зна́ю тако́го краси́вого го́рода, как Пари́ж.
I do not know a city as beautiful as Paris.

Для таки́х люде́й, как он, наде́жды нет.
For people like him there is no hope.

Де́вушка с чёрными, как смоль, волоса́ми.
A young girl with jet-black hair.

When, however, the second element refers to the same person or thing as the first, it agrees with this first word:

Я говорю́ с ва́ми, как друг.   *I am talking to you as a friend.*

Я говорю́ с ва́ми, как с дру́гом.   *I am talking to you as to a friend.*

(v) *As . . . as* is **тако́й же . . . как (и)** or **так же . . . как (и)**:

Он тако́й же высо́кий, как вы.   *He is as tall as you.*

Он рабо́тает так же усе́рдно, как его́ брат.
He works as hard as his brother.

Шторм был не так си́лен, как мне показа́лось.[1]

The gale was not as severe as I had thought.

See also §32.

NOTE:

Приходи́те как мо́жно скоре́е (возмо́жно скоре́е, как то́лько смо́жете).

Come as soon as possible.

Бери́те, ско́лько хоти́те.

Take as much as you like.

Наско́лько я зна́ю (наско́лько мне изве́стно).

As far as I know.

Он проводи́л меня́ до ста́нции.

He went with me as far as the station.

Ещё в девятна́дцатом ве́ке.

As far back as (already in) the nineteenth century.

что каса́ется меня́   *as for me*

§174   ASK

(i) **Спра́шивать/спроси́ть**, *to ask (questions)*[2]; **вопро́с**, *a question*:

Он спроси́л меня́, куда́ я иду́ (е́ду).

He asked me where I was going.

Не спра́шивайте меня́, что́ случи́лось.

Don't ask me what happened.

If *to ask* is followed by a direct object, **y** + *gen.* is used with the person asked:

Он спроси́л у меня́ доро́гу на ста́нцию.

He asked me the way to the station.

Задава́ть/зада́ть вопро́с + *dat.* is used for *to ask a question*:

Ма́льчики за́дали ему́ мно́го вопро́сов.

The boys asked him many questions.

(ii) **Проси́ть/по–** + *gen.* or *acc.*, *to ask for something*; **про́сьба**, *a request*:

Он попроси́л газе́ту.   *He asked for the paper.*

---

[1] Note that **же** is not used in negative constructions.
[2] Вас кто́-то спра́шивал.   *Somebody asked to see you.*

Он попросил меня показать ему дорогу на станцию.
He asked me to show him the way to the station.

Он попросил, чтобы ему не мешали.
He asked not to be disturbed.

У + *gen.* is used of the person asked, if followed by the object asked for:

Он попросил у меня помощи.   *He asked me for help.*

but: Он попросил меня помочь ему.   *He asked me to help him.*

Просить/по– often means *to request* or *to invite*:

Меня попросили подождать.   *I was asked to wait.*

Здесь просят не курить.   *You are requested not to smoke here.*

просить/по– разрешения   *to ask for permission*

просить/по– у кого-нибудь прощения   *to ask somebody's pardon*

§175 CALL, NAME

(i) **Звать** (*impfv.*) with proper names is normally used with the nominative, although (in the past and future) the instrumental is also found. This verb is used only with Christian names and patronymics:

Как вас зовут? (Как ваше имя?)   *What is your name?*

Меня зовут Федя (Таня) or Моё имя — Федя (Таня).
I am called Fedya (Tanya).

Как вас зовут по имени-отчеству? or Как ваше имя-отчество?
What is your Christian name and patronymic?

Меня зовут (по имени-отчеству) Фёдор Петрович (Татьяна Петровна) or Моё имя-отчество — Фёдор Петрович (Татьяна Петровна).
My Christian name and patronymic is Fyodor Petrovich (Tatyana Petrovna).

Как ваша фамилия?   *What is your surname?*

Моя фамилия — Сомов (Сомова).   *My surname is Somov (Somova).*

(ii) **Называть/назвать** used with proper names means *to call* or *to name*. **Называться/назваться** is not used with proper names (see below, iv):

143

Роди́тели назва́ли сы́на Ива́ном.
The parents called their son Ivan.

До свое́й сме́рти никто́ не мо́жет назва́ться счастли́вым.
No man can be called happy before his death.

Плеха́нова ча́сто называ́ют отцо́м ру́сского маркси́зма.
Plekhanov is often called the Father of Russian Marxism.

«Кто там?» — Я назва́л своё и́мя.
'Who is there?' — I gave my name.

(iii) **Звать/по–** is also used in the other sense *to call*[1]:

Когда́ я верну́лся домо́й, оте́ц позва́л меня́ к себе́ в кабине́т.
When I returned home, my father called me into his study.

(iv) **Называ́ть(ся)/назва́ть(ся)** is used of inanimate objects:

Как называ́ется э́тот го́род (э́та у́лица, э́то зда́ние, э́тот рома́н)?
What is this town (street, building, novel) called?

Э́то зда́ние называ́ется (называ́ют) «Дворцо́м культу́ры».
This building is called the Palace of Culture.

Э́тот но́вый райо́н Москвы́ назва́ли Черёмушки.
This new district of Moscow has been named Cheryomushky.

§176   CAN, COULD; MAY, MIGHT; WOULD

(i) **Мочь/с–**, *to be able*; **уме́ть/с–**, *to know how to*:

Я не уме́ю говори́ть по-италья́нски (потому́ что не учи́лся италья́нскому языку́).
I cannot speak Italian (because I have not studied Italian).

Я не уме́ю петь (потому́ что не брал уро́ков).
I cannot sing (because I have not had lessons).

Я не могу́ петь (так как го́рло боли́т).
I cannot sing (as I have a sore throat).

Уме́ете ли вы игра́ть в кри́кет?
Can you play cricket?

Мо́жете ли вы игра́ть в кри́кет за́втра?
Can you play cricket tomorrow?

(ii) **Мочь/с–** also means *can, be allowed*:

Хорошо́, мо́жете идти́.   *All right, you can go.*

---

[1] It is also used meaning *to invite*: Друзья́ зову́т меня́ к себе́ в го́сти, *my friends are inviting (asking) me to go and stay with them.*

Where **мочь/с–** is ambiguous, **мо́жно** is used meaning *can, may*:

Вско́ре по́сле опера́ции он мог ходи́ть.
Soon after the operation he was able to walk about.

Вско́ре по́сле опера́ции ему́ мо́жно бы́ло (= разреши́ли) ходи́ть.
Soon after the operation he was allowed to walk about.

Возмо́жно (negative **невозмо́жно**) means physical ability:

возмо́жно войти́   *there is nothing to prevent one from entering*
мо́жно войти́   *you may enter*

The negative of **мо́жно** is **нельзя́**. After **нельзя́** infinitives in both aspects are found; with an imperfective infinitive **нельзя́** means *it is not allowed*, with a perfective infinitive *it is impossible* (cf. **невозмо́жно**):

По э́той доро́ге нельзя́ проезжа́ть.
You are not allowed to drive along this road.

По э́той доро́ге нельзя́ (невозмо́жно) прое́хать.
It is impossible to drive along this road.

Больно́му нельзя́ встава́ть.   *The patient is not allowed to get up.*
Больно́му нельзя́ встать.   *The patient is unable to get up.*

NOTE:

С э́тим нельзя́ не
    согласи́ться.   *One cannot but agree with this.*

With this idiom the infinitive is generally perfective.

Distinguish between the following:

Он мо́жет прийти́. (Мо́жет быть он придёт. Возмо́жно, что
    придёт.)
He may come (possibility).

Он мо́жет прийти́. (Ему́ мо́жно прийти́.)
He may come (permission).

Возмо́жно, что он пришёл. (Мо́жет быть он пришёл.)
He may have come (possibility).

Возмо́жно, что он пришёл бы, е́сли бы знал. (Он мо́жет быть
    пришёл бы, е́сли бы знал.)
He might have come, if he had known (conditional).

Не мо́жет быть, что́бы она́ э́то сде́лала. (Она́ не могла́ э́того
    сде́лать.)
She can't possibly have done it (possibility excluded).

Могли бы сказать мне.

You might have told me (reproachfully).

Она не могла этого сделать.

She could not do it, have done it.   (Morally and physically unable.)

Вы тоже могли бы прийти.

You could have come too.

Это может быть интересным; возможно, что это будет интересно.

It could (might) be interesting.

Может быть (возможно), что это было бы интересно.

It could (might) have been interesting.

(iii) *Would, could* in polite expressions. Russian is on the whole more direct than English:

Скажите, пожалуйста, который час. (Вы не можете сказать, который час?)

Could you tell me the time, please?

Подождите, пожалуйста.

Would you wait a moment?

For the habitual use of *would*, see §125; for its use in indirect statement, §§87-8, 90; in conditionals, §118.

§177 CHANGE

(i) **Менять** (*impfv.*), **переменять/-ить**, *to change* or *to exchange*:

Я иду в библиотеку менять книгу.

I am going to the library to change my book.

Он переменил адрес.

He changed his address.

Давайте переменим тему разговора.

Let us change the subject.

(ii) **Менять** (*impfv.*), **изменять/-ить**, *to alter* or *to transform*:

Он меняет (изменяет) свои планы очень часто.

He changes his plans very frequently.

Война изменила всё это.

The war has changed all that.

Листья уже меняли (изменяли) цвет.

The leaves were already changing colour.

146

(iii) **Изменя́ть/-и́ть** + *dat.*, to betray, be unfaithful to:

Он измени́л ро́дине.   *He betrayed his country.*

(iv) **Меня́ться** (*impfv.*), **изменя́ться/-и́ться**, to undergo a change:

Времена́ меня́ются.   *Times are changing.*

Положе́ние измени́лось к   *The situation changed for the*
лу́чшему.   *better.*

Он си́льно измени́лся.   *He had changed very much.*

Переме́на is *change* in all three meanings; **изме́на**, *betrayal*.

(v) **Обме́ниваться/обменя́ться** + *instr.*, to exchange (reciprocal):

Они́ обменя́лись мне́ниями.   *They exchanged opinions.*

Обме́н мне́ниями.   *An exchange of opinions.*

Они́ обменя́лись взгля́дами.   *They glanced at each other.*

NOTE:

переду́мывать/переду́мать	*to change one's mind*
переодева́ться/переоде́ться	*to change clothes*
переса́живаться/пересе́сть, де́лать/с– переса́дку	*to change trains*

§178 ENJOY

(i) **Наслажда́ться/наслади́ться** + *instr.* and **наслажде́ние** have a deeper meaning and are used less indiscriminately than their English equivalents *enjoy, enjoyment*:

наслажда́ться/наслади́ться красото́й приро́ды, му́зыкой
to delight in the beauties of nature, to enjoy music

(ii) Other ways of rendering *to enjoy*:

Мы все увлекли́сь его́ исполне́нием сона́ты.[1]
We all enjoyed (were carried away by) his playing of the sonata.

Как вам понра́вилась кни́га? — Она́ мне о́чень понра́вилась.
(Я с удово́льствием чита́л её.)
How did you enjoy the book? I enjoyed it very much. (I enjoyed reading it very much.)

Мы о́чень хорошо́ провели́ вре́мя. (Нам бы́ло о́чень ве́село.)
We thoroughly enjoyed ourselves.

---

[1] Он увлека́ется спо́ртом. *He is keen on sport.*

147

Он испы́тывал удово́льствие, бродя́ по пусты́нным у́лицам
го́рода.
He enjoyed roaming through the deserted streets of the town.

Он по́льзуется хоро́шим здоро́вьем (всео́бщим уваже́нием).
He enjoys good health (universal respect).

§179 FAST, QUICK

(i) **Бы́стрый** is *quick, rapid*, of movements, speech, etc.:

Вы говори́те о́чень бы́стро.	*You speak very quickly.*
бы́строе движе́ние	*a quick movement*

Быстрота́, too, implies great speed:

с быстрото́й мо́лнии	*with lightning speed*

(ii) **Ско́рый, ско́рость** (*f.*), do not necessarily imply great speed
(**ско́ро** means *soon*):

ско́рый по́езд	*a fast train*
ско́рая по́мощь	*first aid*
Уме́ньшите ско́рость!	*Slow down!*
сре́дняя ско́рость	*average speed*

Compare:

как мо́жно быстре́е	*as quickly as possible*
как мо́жно скоре́е	*as soon as possible*

§180 FEEL

(i) **Чу́вствовать/по–**:

чу́вствовать (испы́тывать) ра́дость, сожале́ние, и т. д.
to feel (experience) joy, pity, etc.

Вы что́-нибудь чу́вствуете? — Нет, я ничего́ не чу́вствую.
Can you feel anything? No, I can't feel anything.

Чу́вствовать/по– себя́:

Как вы чу́вствуете себя́?	*How do you feel?*
Я чу́вствую себя́ прекра́сно (лу́чше).	*I feel fine (better).*

Чу́вствоваться/по– (*pass.*), *can be felt*:

Чу́вствовалась не́которая напряжённость.
A certain tension could be felt.

148

(ii) **Испы́тывать/испыта́ть**, *to feel, experience*; **пережива́ть/пере-жи́ть**, *to feel, endure*:

При на́шей сле́дующей встре́че мы о́ба испыта́ли ещё бо́лее о́строе удово́льствие.
We both felt even more pleasure at our next meeting.

Она́ э́то стра́шно пережива́ет. *She feels this very keenly.*

В тече́ние про́шлой войны́ ленингра́дцы пережи́ли стра́шную оса́ду.
During the last war the people of Leningrad endured a terrible siege.

(iii) **Беспоко́иться/о–**, *to feel worried*; **волнова́ться/вз–**, *to feel excited, nervous*:

Она́ о́чень беспоко́илась. *She felt very worried.*

Не беспоко́йтесь! *Don't worry!*

Актри́са о́чень волнова́лась пе́ред выступле́нием.
The actress felt very nervous before she went on stage.

(iv) **Ду́мать/по–**, **каза́ться/по–** + *dat.*, *to feel, to think*:

Я поду́мал (мне показа́лось), что э́то о́чень несправедли́во.
I felt that this was very unfair.

See also §172.

(v) **Хоте́ть(ся)/за–**, *to feel* (hungry, etc.), *to feel like*:

Вы хоти́те поку́шать (=вы го́лодны)? — Нет, но (мне) хо́чется попи́ть. (вы́пить, *to have an alcoholic drink*)
Do you feel hungry? No, but I feel like a drink.

Мне хоте́лось (захоте́лось) погуля́ть.
I felt like going for a walk.

For *to feel warm, cold, happy, sad*, etc., see §137.

§181 GET, REACH

(i) **Получа́ть/–и́ть** has little active force, *to receive*:

Э́то письмо́ я получи́л по по́чте. *I received this letter by post.*

Он получи́л ме́сяц о́тпуска. *He had a month's holiday.*

(ii) **Достава́ть/доста́ть** suggests action by the subject, *to obtain, to go and get, to take out*, etc.:

Э́ту кни́гу я доста́л в библиоте́ке.
I got this book in the library.

Я доста́л (взял) кни́гу с кни́жной по́лки.
I took a book from the bookshelf.

(iii) **Приобрета́ть/приобрести́**, *to acquire, to gain*:

приобрета́ть/приобрести́ позна́ния, друзе́й, иму́щество
to gain knowledge, to win friends, to acquire property

(iv) **Достига́ть/дости́гнуть (дости́чь)** + *gen.* and **добива́ться/ доби́ться** + *gen.* imply considerable effort (*reach, achieve, win*):

В 1959-ом году́ сове́тская раке́та дости́гла луны́.
In 1959 a Soviet rocket reached the moon.

добива́ться/доби́ться своего́ (свое́й це́ли)
to achieve one's aim

доби́ться дове́рия, побе́ды
to win confidence, to gain a victory

For **добива́ться**, *to strive for*, see § 94.

(v) **Добира́ться/добра́ться** + *gen.*, *to reach* (physically), *get through to*[1]:

Они́ с трудо́м добрали́сь до бе́рега.
They reached the shore with difficulty.

(vi) **Попада́ть/попа́сть** is used conversationally for **приходи́ть/ прийти́, очути́ться**, etc.:

Как вы попа́ли сюда́?
How did you get here?

Скажи́те, пожа́луйста, как (мне) попа́сть (= пройти́) на вокза́л.
Could you tell me how to get to the station?

Мы попа́ли во́-время (= успе́ли) на по́езд.
We caught the train.

Он попа́л в дурно́е о́бщество.
He got into bad company.

Note also:

Он попа́л ного́й в лу́жу.	*He stepped into a puddle.*
Он не мог попа́сть ключо́м в замо́к.	*He could not get the key into the lock.*

---

[1] **Доноси́ться/донести́сь** + *gen.*, *to reach, drift up to*, is used of sounds, etc.:

До нас доноси́лись отдалённые зву́ки му́зыки.
The sounds of distant music drifted up to us.

(vii) **(Дозва́ниваться)/дозвони́ться** + *gen.*, *to get through to* (by telephone):

Вчера́ я вам звони́л, но нельзя́ бы́ло дозвони́ться.
I rang you yesterday, but could not get through.

(viii) *To get someone to do something* is **заставля́ть/заста́вить кого́-нибудь сде́лать что́-нибудь**:

Мы заста́вили шофёра поверну́ть наза́д.
We got the driver to turn back.

NOTE:

отдава́ть/отда́ть ту́фли в ремо́нт (в почи́нку)	*to get shoes repaired*
отдава́ть/отда́ть прояви́ть плёнки	*to get films developed*

§182 GO

Я ходи́л за поку́пками.   *I went shopping.*

Зимо́й мы ката́емся на конька́х (на лы́жах, на саня́х/на саля́зках[1]).
In the winter we go skating (skiing, sledging).

Мы ча́сто ката́емся верхо́м (на ло́дке).
We often go riding (boating).

Вчера́ днём мы ходи́ли гуля́ть (мы прогуля́лись, сде́лали прогу́лку).   *Yesterday afternoon we went for a walk.*

Мы идём на прогу́лку (е́дем на экску́рсию; соверша́ем прогу́лку, экску́рсию).
We are going on an outing.

Я хожу́ ка́ждый день в шко́лу (see §184).
I go to school every day.

Мы заходи́ли/заезжа́ли к дру́гу.   *We went to see my friend.*

Вот раздаётся звоно́к. (Звоно́к.)   *There goes the bell.*

See also Verbs of Motion, §§127-35.

§183 HAVE

(i) **У меня́** (etc.) + *nom.*:

У меня́ два бра́та.   *I have two brothers.*

У них была́ но́вая кварти́ра.   *They had a new flat.*

---

[1] **Са́ни** is a large, horse-drawn sledge, **саля́зки** a child's sledge.

У меня болит голова.   *I have a headache.*

For **у меня** in a negative statement, see §141.

(ii) **Иметь** + *acc.* Its primary meaning is *to have, own*: **он имеет свой дом, свою машину,** but it is used in an abstract sense, e.g.:

иметь возможность (случай, надежду и т.д.)
to have an opportunity (occasion, hope, etc.)

Понятия не имею.   *I have no idea.*

Note also:

Мы пили чай в саду.	*We had tea in the garden.*
Мы хорошо поговорили (see §95, i).	*We had a good talk.*
Мальчики выкупались в озере.	*The boys had a swim in the lake.*
Он, казалось, испытывал затруднения в переводе.	*He seemed to have difficulties with the translating.*
Мне нужно постричь себе волосы.	*I must have a hair-cut.*
Мы хорошо провели время (see §178).	*We had a good time.*
Нам ещё далеко идти.	*We still have a long way to go.*
Ну, как хотите!	*Have it your own way.*
Мне нужно (надо) идти (see §189).	*I have to go now.*
Скажите, чтобы отнесли мои вещи ко мне в комнату.	*Have my things taken to my room.*

(iii) With inanimate subjects avoid **у** + *gen.*:

В Лондоне больше сорока театров.
London has over forty theatres.

При этой школе хорошая столовая.
This school has a good canteen.

В нашем доме только одна ванная.
Our house has only one bathroom.

Вокруг (около) дома сад. (За домом сад.)
This house has a garden.

For *this house has no garden*, **этот дом без сада** is better than **у этого дома нет сада.**

§184 LEARN, STUDY

(i) Учи́ться/вы́-, на-, + *dat.*

To learn, not necessarily academic subjects:

В шко́ле (на вече́рних ку́рсах) мы у́чимся францу́зскому языку́.
We are learning French at school (in evening classes).

Я научи́лся францу́зскому языку́.
I learnt French (completed a course of French).

Я научи́лся води́ть маши́ну (пла́вать, е́здить верхо́м).
I learnt to drive a car (to swim, to ride).

To go to school, be a pupil[1]:

Где ты у́чишься? — Я учу́сь в сре́дней шко́ле.
Which school do you go to? I go to a secondary school.

but:

Мы хо́дим ка́ждый день в шко́лу (see §128).
We go to school every day.

To be studying (see also **занима́ться**, below):

Что де́лает Джон? — Он у́чится.
What's John doing? He is working (studying).

(ii) Учи́ть/вы́- +*acc.*, *to learn* (a specific topic of study)[2]:

Я вы́учил уро́к.   *I did my homework.*

Я вы́учил стихотворе́ние наизу́сть.   *I learnt a poem by heart.*

(iii) Изуча́ть/-и́ть +*acc.*, *to study an academic subject*:

Мы изуча́ем ру́сскую исто́рию.
We are studying Russian history.

Мой брат изуча́л фи́зику в университе́те.
My brother did (took, read) physics at the University.

Он изучи́л фи́зику suggests a high level of competence. Note that **изуча́ть/-и́ть** is ALWAYS followed by a direct object.

---

[1] *To start (going to) school* is **поступа́ть/-и́ть в шко́лу**:
В про́шлом году́ моя́ сестра́ поступи́ла в шко́лу.
To go to secondary school, where a transfer is involved, is **переходи́ть/ перейти́ в сре́днюю шко́лу**.

[2] **Учи́ть/вы́-** can also mean *to study academically*, cf. **изуча́ть/-и́ть**; **учи́ть исто́рию**, *to study history*. Contrast: **он у́чит фи́зику**, *he is reading physics* and **он у́чит фи́зике**, *he teaches physics* (see §197).

(iv) **Занима́ться** + *instr.*, *to be working, studying* (cf. **учи́ться**):

Вчера́ я занима́лся весь день.
Yesterday I was working all day.

По суббо́там у нас в шко́ле не занима́ются (не быва́ет заня́тий).
We have no school on Saturdays.

§185 LEAVE, LET

(i) *To leave, go away, go out, depart,* **уходи́ть/уйти́, уезжа́ть/ уе́хать, выходи́ть/вы́йти, выезжа́ть/вы́ехать,** etc.:

Когда́ мы пришли́, он уже́ ушёл.
He had already left when we came.

Он уе́хал (вы́ехал) в дере́вню.	*He left for the country.*
Вчера́ он уе́хал (вы́ехал) из А́нглии.	*He left England yesterday.*
Он ти́хо вы́шел из ко́мнаты.	*He left the room quietly.*
Когда́ по́езд отхо́дит?	*When does the train leave?*

See also §135.

To leave (behind), **оставля́ть/оста́вить:**

Я оста́вил кни́ги до́ма.   *I left my books at home.*

По́сле э́того нас оста́вили в поко́е.
They left us in peace after that.

Мы оста́вили дете́й до́ма.   *We left the children at home.*

Кто́-то оста́вил для вас запи́ску.   *Someone left a note for you.*

Э́то мы пока́ оста́вим.   *We'll leave this for now.*

Война́ оста́вила на нём следы́.
The war has left its mark on him.

To leave permanently, abandon, **оставля́ть/оста́вить, покида́ть/ поки́нуть:**

Ей пришло́сь навсегда́ оста́вить (поки́нуть) роди́тельский дом.
She had to leave her home for ever.

Оста́вь нас, го́рдый челове́к! [Пу́шкин]
Leave us, proud man!

See also §194(i).

(ii) *Let, allow,* **позволя́ть/-и́ть, разреша́ть/-и́ть** + *dat.*:

Мы позво́лили ему́ уйти́.   *We let him go.*

Доктор разрешил ему встать с постели.
The doctor let him get up.

Я не позволю вам говорить об этом.
I won't let you talk about this.

Позвольте заметить вам, что вы ошибаетесь.
Let me tell you that you are wrong.

Let's is rendered (*a*) by the first person plural (*pres.* or *fut.pfv.*) without мы: идём (пойдём) в город (or, more courteous: идёмте, пойдёмте); (*b*) by давайте+1st *pers.pl.*: давайте почитаем эту книгу, давайте побеседуем; (*c*) by давайте + *infin.*: давайте читать, давайте беседовать.

Let him, etc., пусть (пускай) + *pres.* or *fut.pfv.*:

Пусть он делает, что хочет.	*Let him do what he likes.*
Пусть он придёт.	*Let him come.*

NOTE:

Мы дали им волю.	*We let them loose.*
Я дам вам знать.	*I'll let you know.*
Дайте мне кончить.	*Let me finish.*
Комната сдаётся.	*Room to let.*

§186 LIKE, LOVE

(i) **Любить/по–**, *to love, be fond of.* It also means *to like*, when this describes a preference that has become a habit:

Я люблю зиму (свою работу, водку, русские папиросы).
I like the winter (my work, vodka, Russian cigarettes).

Note the constructions:

Я люблю, чтобы во всём был порядок.
I like there to be order in everything.

Я не люблю, когда мне мешают за работой (cf. §114).
I don't like being disturbed at my work.

Он любит, *he is in love*, expresses a profounder feeling than **он влюблён**.

(ii) **Нравиться/по–** expresses an initial favourable impression created by a person or thing:

Мне не нравится этот человек.	*I don't like (the look of) this man.*

but:

Я не люблю́ э́того челове́ка.   *I don't like (care for) this man.*

Compare also:

Вчера́ я прочита́л расска́зы Толсто́го; они́ мне о́чень по-
нра́вились.
I read some stories of Tolstoy yesterday; I liked them very much.

Я о́чень люблю́ расска́зы Толсто́го.
I like Tolstoy's stories very much.

Вчера́шний конце́рт понра́вился нам всем.
We all liked yesterday's concert.

Мы все лю́бим (му́зыку) Мо́царта.
All of us like Mozart.

Снача́ла ру́сский стол мне во́все не нра́вился, но постепе́нно
я полюби́л его́; тепе́рь да́же о́чень люблю́ его́.
*At first I did not like Russian cooking at all, but gradually I became
quite fond of it; now I like it very much.*

A visitor to England might say:
Мне (не) нра́вится англи́йский кли́мат.

After some time in the country he might say:
Я (не) люблю́ англи́йский кли́мат.

NOTE:

Хоти́те ча́ю?   *Would you like some tea?*

Я хоте́л бы пое́хать в Росси́ю.   *I would like to go to Russia.*

§187 LOOK, WATCH

(i) Смотре́ть/по–

With в and на + *acc.*, to look at:

Он посмотре́л (взгляну́л) на меня́.   *He looked at me.*

Он посмотре́л в кни́гу.   *He looked at (into) the book.*

With plain accusative or как and subordinate clause, *to watch, to see*:

(по)смотре́ть футбо́льный матч (телеви́зор, пье́су, кинофи́льм)
to watch a football match (television, a play, a film)

(по)смотре́ть дом   *to look over a house*

156

Мать смотре́ла, как ребёнок чита́ет (чита́л) кни́гу.
The mother watched the child reading its book.

With **за** + *instr.*, *to look after*:

(по)смотре́ть за детьми́ (за больны́ми)	*to look after children* (*patients*)
(по)смотре́ть за поря́дком	*to keep order*

(ii) **Осма́тривать/осмотре́ть**, *to look at, to examine*:

Мы пошли́ осмотре́ть го́род.
We went to have a look at the town.

До́ктор ка́ждый день осма́тривал больно́го.
The doctor examined the patient every day.

(iii) **Наблюда́ть** (*impfv.*)

With plain accusative or **как** and subordinate clause, *to watch, to observe*:

Нас внима́тельно наблюда́л челове́к в друго́м купе́.
A man in the other compartment was watching us closely.

Он наблюда́л, как мы раскла́дывали свои́ чемода́ны.
He watched us unpack our suitcases.

With **за** + *instr.*, *to watch, to supervise*:

За у́личным движе́нием наблюда́л милиционе́р.
A policeman was supervising the traffic.

(iv) **Следи́ть** (*impfv.*) **за** + *instr.*, *to watch, follow* (with one's eyes or mentally):

Мы внима́тельно следи́ли за ка́ждым его́ движе́нием.
We closely watched his every movement.

следи́ть за диску́ссией   *to follow, keep up with the discussion*

(v) **Вы́глядеть** (*impfv.*), *to look, appear*; **быть похо́жим на** + *acc.*, *to look like*:

Он вы́глядел ве́село.	*He looked cheerful.*
Дом вы́глядит совсе́м но́вым.	*The house looks quite new.*
Он о́чень похо́ж на бра́та.	*He is very much like his brother.*

157

§188 MEAN

(i) **Значить,** *to mean, to signify*:

Что значит это слово?   *What does this word mean?*

Значит is sometimes interpolated:

Вы готовы? Значит, можно идти.

Are you ready? Then we can go.

(ii) **Хотеть сказать,** *to mean* (cf. French *vouloir dire*):

Что вы хотите этим сказать?   *What do you mean by this?*

§189 MUST, HAVE TO, NEED, OUGHT, SHOULD

(i) **Должен (должна, должны)** + *infin.* is a predicative adjective implying a duty or moral obligation. It also means *is intended to be, is due*:

Как члены Комсомола мы должны подавать хороший пример.

As members of the Komsomol we must set a good example.

Вы должны понять это.   *You must understand this.*

Этот парк должен был быть украшением города.

This park was to be an adornment to the town.

Поезд должен был прибыть в девять часов.

The train was due to arrive at nine o'clock.

(ii) **Надо (нужно)** + *dat.* and *infin.* suggests necessity or desirability rather than obligation:

Вы идёте с нами в город? — Не могу, мне надо (нужно) работать.

Are you coming with us to town? I can't, I have to work.

Надо было сказать мне об этом раньше.

You should have told me about that sooner.

Надо and **нужно** can also express the means to an end:

Чтобы сдать экзамен, надо много работать.

In order to pass the examination you have to work hard.

(iii) **Нужен (нужна, нужно, нужны)** is the predicative form of **нужный**. It means *necessary* and is used to translate *I need*, etc.:

Это очень нужная работа.   *This is very necessary* (i.e. *important*) *work.*

Мне нужен новый костюм.   *I need a new suit.*

Мне нужны были деньги.   *I needed some money.*

158

(iv) **Прихо́дится (приходи́лось/пришло́сь, придётся)** + *dat.* and *infin.* suggests an unpleasant result, a nuisance:

Так как у меня́ не́ было де́нег, мне пришло́сь оста́ться до́ма.
Since I had no money, I had to stay at home.

It may also mean *I happened to, I had occasion to*:

Одна́жды мне пришло́сь (случи́лось) е́хать по Во́лге.
One day I happened to be travelling along the Volga.

(v) **Сле́дует, сле́довало (бы)**, *ought, should*, is less direct than **до́лжен**:

Вам сле́дует (сле́довало) знать э́то.
You should know (should have known) this.

Вам сле́дует (сле́довало бы) быть бо́лее осторо́жным.
You ought to be more careful.

NOTE:

Сиди́те как сле́дует.   *Sit properly.*

Вы́ругал я его́ как сле́дует.   *I gave him a good telling off.*

See also under Subjunctive, §115.

(vi) **Должно́ быть** is used parenthetically like **мо́жет быть** to express probability.[1] It is similar in meaning to **наве́рное, очеви́дно**:

Он должно́ быть (наве́рное) ждал вас с утра́.
He must have waited for you since morning.

Должно́ быть (должно́ быть бы́ло) по́здно.
It must be (must have been) late.

Очеви́дно (должно́ быть) он в библиоте́ке.
He must be in the library.

Мы сейча́с наве́рное приближа́емся к свое́й це́ли.
We must be reaching our destination now.

§190 NEXT

(i) **Сле́дующий**, *following*, is used especially with the past tense:

В сле́дующем году́ они́ пое́хали в Москву́.
The next year they went to Moscow.

---

[1] Note the difference between они́ должно́ быть до́ма, *they must be (probably are) at home*, and они́ должны́ быть до́ма, *they must be (are bound to be) at home*.

Мы сойдём на следующей остановке.
We are getting off at the next stop.

(ii) **Будущий** is not used with the past tense:

В будущем году мы едем в Москву.
Next year we are going to Moscow.

(iii) **Другой** is used in certain expressions of time:

на другой день, на другое утро
the next day, next morning

(iv) **Ближайший** is used in the sense *nearest*:

До ближайшего села было ещё пять миль.
The next village was five miles away.

(v) **Соседний** is used in the sense *adjoining*:

Они были в соседней комнате.   *They were in the next room.*

§191 QUIET, CALM, SILENT

(i) **Тихий**, *quiet, subdued* (of sound) is used as:

(*a*) The opposite of **шумный**:

тихая ночь	*a quiet night*
На улице было тихо.	*It was quiet outside (on the street).*

(*b*) The opposite of **громкий**:

Она говорила тихо (тихим голосом).   *She spoke quietly.*

(*c*) The opposite of **быстрый** (see §179):

тихий ход	*dead slow*
Идите тише! (*coll.*)	*Walk more slowly.*

(ii) **Спокойный**, *quiet, calm*, is the opposite of **бурный**:

спокойное море	*a calm sea*
спокойная погода	*calm weather*

NOTE:

Спокойной ночи!	*Good night.*
Сиди спокойно!	*Sit still!*

It is also used as the opposite of **тревожный**, to suggest inward calm:

Она слушала это известие спокойно.
She listened to this news calmly.

160

(iii) **Неслы́шный** is *inaudible*:

неслы́шные шаги́ — *silent footsteps*

(iv) **Мо́лча** is *silently, in silence*:

Они́ стоя́ли мо́лча. — *They stood in silence.*

NOTE:

Молчи́(те)! (Молча́ть! Ти́ше!) — *Keep quiet!*

§192 SAY, SPEAK, TALK, TELL

(i) **Говори́ть/по-** is followed by **с** + *instr.* of the person addressed, and means *to speak, to talk*:

Он хорошо́ говори́т по-ру́сски. — *He speaks Russian well.*

О чём вы с ним говори́ли? — *What did you talk to him about?*

Мы хорошо́ поговори́ли. — *We had a good talk.*

Говори́те гро́мче! — *Speak up!*

(ii) **Говори́ть/сказа́ть** + *dat.* of the person addressed is *to say, to tell* (of limited statements):

Что вы сказа́ли? — *What did you say?*

Я сказа́л дру́гу, что мы бы́ли за грани́цей.
I told my friend that we had been abroad.

Скажи́те, пожа́луйста, кото́рый час.
Tell me the time, please.

Не говори́те ему́ ничего́. — *Don't tell him anything.*

Я вам об э́том говори́л вчера́. — *I told you about this yesterday.*

Тру́дно сказа́ть. — *It is hard to tell.*

See also §98.

(iii) **Расска́зывать/рассказа́ть** + *dat.* of the person addressed is *to tell, to narrate, to give an account*:

Расскажи́те о себе́. — *Tell me about yourself.*

Я расска́зывал дру́гу о том, что мы ви́дели за грани́цей.
I was telling my friend what we had seen abroad.

Он хорошо́ расска́зывает анекдо́ты.
He is good at telling jokes.

(iv) **Разгова́ривать** (no *pfv.*) means *to converse*:

Не разгова́ривать! — *No talking!*

161

§193 SINCE

(i) Temporal: **с** + *gen.* (*prp.*); **с тех пор** (*adv.*); **с тех пор, как** (*conj.*):

С про́шлого го́да я не ви́дел его́.
I have not seen him since last year.

С тех пор я не ви́дел его́.
I have not seen him since.

Прошла́ неде́ля с тех пор, я как ви́дел его́ в после́дний раз.
It is a week since I saw him last.

(ii) Causal: **так как** (*conj.*):

Он не мог прийти́, так как был бо́лен.
He could not come, since he was ill.

§194 STAY

(i) **Остава́ться/оста́ться**, *to remain, to stay behind, to be left*:

Оста́ньтесь здесь, пока́ я не верну́сь.	*Stay here till I return.*
Го́сти ушли́, и я оста́лся оди́н.	*The guests left, and I was left alone.*
У меня́ не оста́лось ни копе́йки.	*I had not a penny left.*

NOTE:

Он оста́лся дово́лен их рабо́той.
He was pleased with their work.

Никто́ не оста́лся в живы́х по́сле круше́ния самолёта.
No one survived the plane crash.

(ii) **Сиде́ть/по– до́ма**, *to stay at home*:

Он сиди́т до́ма весь день.
He stays at home all day.

(iii) **Остана́вливаться/останови́ться**, *to stay, put up at*:

Я всегда́ остана́вливаюсь в гости́нице «Ритц» (в «Ри́тце»).
I always stay at the 'Ritz'.

Я останови́лся в гости́нице «Метропо́ль» (в «Метропо́ле»).
I was staying (i.e. put up) at the 'Metropole'.

(iv) **Жить/по– (про–)**, *to stay at somebody's place, to live with*:

У кого́ вы живёте? — Я живу́ у бра́та.
With whom are you staying? I am staying with my brother.

162

(v) **Гостить**, *stay with, visit*:

Я гостил у друзей в деревне.
I was staying with friends in the country.

(vi) **Пробыть** (*pfv.*), *to stay, to spend some time*:

Сколько времени вы пробыли в Париже? — Я пробыл там три недели.
How long did you stay in Paris? I stayed there for three weeks.

§195 STOP

(i) **Останавливать(ся)/остановить(ся)**, *to stop, to halt*:

Шофёр остановил машину.	*The driver stopped the car.*
Меня остановил милиционер.	*I was stopped by a policeman.*
Машина остановилась.	*The car stopped.*

(ii) **Переставать/перестать**, *to stop, to cease*:

Он перестал говорить.	*He stopped speaking.*
Дождь перестал (идти).	*It stopped raining.*

(iii) **Прекращать(ся)/прекратить(ся)**, *to stop, to break off*:

После этого письма наша переписка прекратилась.
After this letter our correspondence stopped.

Оба государства прекратили дипломатические отношения.
The two countries broke off diplomatic relations.

(iv) **Стоять/по– (про–)**, *to stop, to be stationary*:

Здесь поезд стоит пять минут.
The train stops here for five minutes.

Стой(те)! Постой(те)!
Stop!

(v) **Удерживать/удержать**, *to stop, to restrain*; **удерживаться/удержаться**, *to refrain*:

Я не мог удержать его от этого необдуманного шага.
I could not stop him from taking this ill-considered step.

Он еле удержался от слёз.
He could scarcely hold back his tears.

(vi) **Положить** (*pfv.*) **чему-нибудь конец**, *to put a stop to something*:

Этому делу положим конец.   *We'll put a stop to this.*

163

§196 TAKE

Брать/взять is the usual translation with inanimate objects:

Он взял зóнтик.	*He took his umbrella.*
Берúте, скóлько хотúте.	*Take as much as you like.*
У когó вы взя́ли дéньги?	*From whom did you take the money?*

It can also be used with persons as *to take someone along*:

Мы взя́ли мáльчика с собóй на экскýрсию.
We took the boy with us on the outing.

For the use of verbs of motion as translation of *to take*, see §§ 127, 130.

Note the following:

принимáть/приня́ть лекáрство	*to take medicine*
принимáть/приня́ть учáстие, во внимáние	*to take part, into account*
дéлать/с– шагú	*to take steps*
снимáть/снять кóмнату	*to take (rent) a room*
нанимáть/наня́ть таксú (see also §130).	*to take (hire) a taxi*
Я вас прúнял за другóго.	*I took you to be someone else.*
Всё э́то занимáет врéмя.	*All this takes time.*
Путешéствие продолжáлось три часá.	*The journey took three hours.*
Мы шли (éхали) тудá три часá.	*It took us three hours to get there.*
Он не торопúлся.	*He took his time.*
Он измéрил мне температýру.	*He took my temperature.*

§197 TEACH

(i) **Учúть/на–** + *dat.* of subject taught and *acc./gen.* of persons taught:

Он ýчит детéй матемáтике (францýзскому языкý).
He teaches the children Maths (French).

Also in the non-academic sense:

Он учúл меня́ плáванию и ездé верхóм.
He taught me swimming and riding.

With the infinitive:

Он учи́л меня́ говори́ть по-францу́зски (игра́ть в ка́рты).
He taught me to speak French (to play cards).

(ii) **Преподава́ть** + *acc.* of the subject and *dat.* of the person taught; it suggests specialised teaching:

Профе́ссор Ивано́в преподаёт студе́нтам францу́зский язы́к.
Professor Ivanov teaches the students French.

Он преподаёт дре́внюю исто́рию в университе́те.
He teaches Ancient History at the University.

Здесь преподаётся англи́йский язы́к.
English is taught here.

(iii) **Учи́ть, преподава́ть**, *to teach, to be a teacher*:

Мой оте́ц у́чит (преподаёт) в сре́дней шко́ле.
My father teaches at a secondary school.

Cf. §184.

§198 TURN

(i) **Верте́ть (верчу́, ве́ртишь)/по–, враща́ть** (*impfv.*), *to spin, to cause to rotate*:

верте́ть тро́сть	*to twirl a cane*
враща́ть колесо́	*to spin a wheel*

(ii) **Верте́ться/по–**, *to spin, rotate*:

Земля́ ве́ртится вокру́г свое́й со́бственной о́си.
The earth rotates round its own axis.

(iii) **Враща́ться**, *to rotate round an object, to orbit*:

Земля́ враща́ется вокру́г со́лнца.
The earth rotates round the sun.

(iv) **Крути́ть (кручу́, кру́тишь)/по–**, *to twist, to turn, to roll*:

крути́ть ру́чку, папиро́су   *to turn a handle, roll a cigarette*

(v) **Крути́ться/по–, кружи́ться/по–, за–**, *to spin, whirl*:

Ли́стья, крутя́сь, па́дали на зе́млю.
The leaves whirled to the ground.

У неё кружи́лась голова́.   *She felt dizzy.*

(vi) **Повора́чивать(ся)/поверну́ть(ся)**, *to turn*; by itself the verb implies no specific direction:

Не дойдя́ до вокза́ла, он поверну́л наза́д и пошёл домо́й.[1]
Before he reached the station, he turned back and went home.

Она́ ме́дленно поверну́ла го́лову ко мне.
She turned her head slowly towards me.

Он поверну́лся ко мне спино́й.   *He turned his back to me.*

Он поверну́лся в сто́рону.   *He turned away, to one side.*

(vii) **Обора́чивать(ся)/оберну́ть(ся)**, *to turn round, to turn to one side*:

Он оберну́лся ко мне.   *He turned round to me.*

Она́ оберну́ла го́лову   *She turned her head away.*
в сто́рону.

Он оберну́лся в ту сто́рону, куда́ она́ смотре́ла.
He turned to see what she was looking at.

(viii) **Отвора́чивать(ся)/отверну́ть(ся)**, *to turn away*:

Он мо́лча отверну́лся.   *He turned away in silence.*

Он отверну́л го́лову.   *He turned his head to one side.*

Отверни́тесь!   *Look the other way!*

(ix) **Завора́чивать/заверну́ть**, *to turn, turn a corner, call in on* or *at*:

Вса́дники заверну́ли лошаде́й наза́д.
The riders turned their horses back.

Маши́на заверну́ла за́ угол.[1]   *The car turned the corner.*

---

[1] Note that **повора́чивать/поверну́ть, завора́чивать/заверну́ть** and **свора́чивать/сверну́ть**, when used intransitively, indicate actions performed while in motion; the intransitive verbs ending in –**ся** indicate actions performed while stationary.
Imperfective forms with the stem –**вёртывать** are also found. Compare **отвора́чивать/отверну́ть** го́лову and **отвёртывать/отверну́ть** кран:
Он отверну́л кран.   *He turned the tap on.*
Заверни́те кран скоре́е!   *Turn the tap off quickly!*
They are also used when the verb has no longer the primary meaning *to turn*, e.g. **завёртывать/заверну́ть, развёртывать/разверну́ть**, *to wrap, unwrap*; **свёртывать/сверну́ть**, *to roll*:
Продаве́ц заверну́л мою́ поку́пку в бума́гу.
The shop assistant wrapped up what I had bought.
Он сверну́л себе́ папиро́су и закури́л (её).
He rolled himself a cigarette and smoked it.

Иногда́ Алёша прое́здом завора́чивал в сосе́днюю дере́вню.[1]
Sometimes Alyosha would call in at the next village on his way.

(x) **Свора́чивать/сверну́ть,** *to turn off, change direction:*

Он сверну́л в переу́лок.[1] *He turned off into a side street.*

(xi) **Обраща́ться/обрати́ться к** + *dat.,* *to turn to, to address, to approach,* etc.:

Он обрати́лся к нам за по́мощью.
He turned to us for help.

Обраща́ясь к кла́ссу, он сказа́л...
Addressing the class he said...

К кому́ мне обрати́ться по э́тому де́лу?
Whom should I see about this?

Note also:

Обрати́те внима́ние (на то), как э́то де́лается (де́лают).
Notice how this is done.

(xii) **Возвраща́ть(ся)/верну́ть(ся),** *to return:*

На́до верну́ть э́ту кни́гу в библиоте́ку.
I have to return this book to the library.

Мы верну́лись с конце́рта о́чень по́здно.
We returned very late from the concert.

The perfective **возврати́ть(ся)** is rarely used in spoken Russian.

§199 WONDER

I wonder is rendered by **я спра́шиваю себя́, я хочу́ знать,** and even **(я) не зна́ю** and **интере́сно** followed by an indirect question:

Она́ спра́шивала себя́, отчего́ (почему́, заче́м) он э́то сде́лал.
She wondered why he had done this.

Он спра́шивал себя́ (хоте́л знать), как э́то могло́ случи́ться.
He wondered how this could have happened.

Я не зна́ю, что де́лать тепе́рь.   *I wonder what to do now.*

Conversationally:

Интере́сно, ско́лько э́то сто́ило.   *I wonder how much it cost.*

Не зна́ю, придёт ли он.   *I wonder if he'll come.*
(Да придёт ли он?)

Cf. §19(ii).

[1] See footnote to p. 166.

§200 WRONG

(i) Неве́рный, непра́вильный:

Э́то неве́рно (непра́вда).	*This is wrong (untrue).*
Э́то непра́вильно.	*This is wrong (incorrect).*
Мои́ часы́ неве́рны, иду́т непра́вильно.	*My watch is wrong.*

(ii) Не тот, не так:

Он пошёл не по той у́лице.	*He took the wrong road.*
Э́то не то сло́во.	*That's the wrong word.*
Вы не так отве́тили. (Ваш отве́т непра́вилен.)	*Your answer is wrong.*

(iii) Нела́дный (*coll.*), wrong, not in order:

Здесь что́-то нела́дно.	*There is something wrong here.*

(iv) Ошиба́ться/–и́ться, to be wrong, mistaken:

Мне ка́жется, что вы ошиба́етесь.	*I think you are mistaken.*
Я оши́бся в до́ме.	*I went to the wrong house.*

NOTE:

Вы напра́сно рассказа́ли им всё.	*It was wrong of you to tell them everything.*

§201 TRANSCRIPTION OF ENGLISH NAMES

Surnames, names of institutions, newspapers, etc. are normally transcribed; that is an approximate rendering is made of the *sound* of the word. Letter-by-letter transliteration is rarely used.

The English *a* is rendered by either **а**, **э**, **е** or **ей**:

А́лан	*Alan*	ле́ди	*Lady*
Гэ́мпшир	*Hampshire*	Джеймс	*James*

E [e] is normally **э** initially and **е** after a consonant; [i:] is **и**:

Э́ллиотт	*Elliott*	Й́ден	*Eden*
Бе́тти	*Betty*		

Ou is **ау**:

Сауте́нд-он-Си   *Southend on Sea*

U is **у** or **а**:

Ву́стер	*Worcester*	Ха́мбер	*Humber*

H is either **x** or **г**:

Халл, Гулль	*Hull*	Геркулéс	*Hercules*
Хэ́мпстед	*Hampstead*	Ги́тлер	*Hitler*

J is **дж**:

Джон	*John*	Джейн	*Jane*

Th is either **т, с** or **з** (**ф** in words of Greek origin):

Смит	*Smith*	Рéзерфорд	*Rutherford*
Голсуóрси	*Galsworthy*	Афи́ны	*Athens*

W is rendered by **у** and sometimes by **в**:

Суóнси	*Swansea*	Уи́льям, Ви́льям	*William*
Уэ́льс	*Wales*	Голливу́д	*Hollywood*
	Уóрнер брáзерс	*Warner Bros.*	

Initial *y* is rendered by **й**:

Нью-Йорк	*New York*

By the process of transcription *Modern Languages, Daily Worker* and *Associated Press* become **Мóдерн лэ́нгуиджиз, Дéйли уóркер, Ассошиэ́йтед пресс.**

Index

Numbers refer to paragraphs throughout. Not all words occurring in groups illustrating the same point are necessarily listed here.

172